THE OSIRIS FACTOR

NEW SOLUTIONS FOR OVERCOMING HUMAN DESTRUCTIVENESS

THE OSIRIS FACTOR

NEW SOLUTIONS
FOR OVERCOMING
HUMAN DESTRUCTIVENESS

by

Philip Roos, Ph.D.

BONNEVILLE BOOKS™
Springville, Utah

ISBN: 1-55517-595-3
v.1

Published by Bonneville Books
Imprint of Cedar Fort Inc.
www.cedarfort.com

Distributed by:

Typeset by Kristin Nelson
Cover design by Adam Ford

Printed in the United States of America
10 9 8 7 6 5 4 3 2 1

Printed on acid-free paper

Library of Congress Cataloging-in-Publication Data

Roos, Philip.
The Osiris Factor : Say good-bye to anger, shame, guilt and depression / by Philip Roos.
p. cm.
Includes bibliographical references.
ISBN 1-55517-595-3 (pbk. : alk. paper)
1. Self-destructive behavior. 2. Judgment. 3. Humility. I. Title.
RC569.5.S45 R66 2002
155.2'32--dc21

2001006989

To Susan and Valerie

ACKNOWLEDGMENTS

This book was made possible by the thousands of clients who shared their lives with me and let me learn from their courage and resourcefulness. From fellow professionals I have gained a wealth of wisdom, much of which is reflected in this book. I particularly want to single out the work of Albert Ellis, Ph.D., Aaron Beck, M.D., Irving Polster, Ph.D., Steven De Shazer, Ph.D., Michael Yapko, Ph.D., and Arnold Lazarus, Ph.D. as having influenced me profoundly.

Special appreciation is due to Shelly Hill, my former Office Manager, who helped with much of the technical manuscript preparation and logistic support during the early stages of this project.

I feel deep appreciation for the support and encouragement of my beloved wife, Susan Roos, Ph.D., herself author of a recent book and a masterful therapist. Many of her insights are reflected in this book. I also thank the staff at Cedar Fort, Inc. for their efforts in bringing this book forth.

I also want to thank my animal companions—Tashka, Mignonne, and Pepy (cats), Caesar (tiger), and Cheatin Heart (horse) for their unconditional love and wisdom.

TABLE OF CONTENTS

FOREWORD

BY LEE NELSON

A day or two after reading the *Osiris Factor* manuscript by Philip Roos I found myself in the drive-up line at the neighborhood Gas-n-Go hoping to purchase a fountain drink to take back to the office where a virtual mountain of unread manuscripts was awaiting my attention.

When I reached the second position I noticed the clerk at the window was engaged in an animated discussion with the customer in the vehicle in front of me. The discussion continued as the drink was handed over, the money received, then the change handed back. But the car remained in place as the discussion continued.

"Now that the service has been rendered, the customer *should* leave," I thought. "The clerk should stop talking so the next customer, me, can be waited on. Can't anybody around this stupid place do anything right?" Nothing happened, other than a continuation of the conversation. I was really angry now.

"They can keep their damn soda. I'll take my business and my cash elsewhere!" I shoved my transmission into reverse, checked the rearview mirror, and was about to stomp on the gas when I remembered some of the words from *The Osiris Factor*. Osiris was an Egyptian god who judged people, frequently unfairly, when they died. The book is about the unnecessary judging we do in our lives, that frequently results in anger, guilt, shame and eventually depression, and how all this can be avoided.

I was *shoulding* the two women in front of me. I had made

a judgment that clerks *should* never continue conversation with customers after service is rendered, and this clerk was in serious non-compliance. I had made a judgment that customers *should* not speak to clerks after service is rendered, and the driver was in serious violation. I was playing god, and felt anger because two women would not comply with my definition of how the universe should function. In *The Osiris Factor*, Roos draws from hundreds if not thousands of clinical case studies to show the need to be less judgmental, and how achieving this results in less anger, guilt, shame and depression. If you know anyone who angers easily, especially over trivial matters like described above, this book could change their life forever.

As much as I wanted to hurry back to work, I had to confess I was unfairly shoulding or judging the two women in front of me. They weren't making me late for anything important. Maybe the woman in the car had buried her husband this week, and the friend at the window was expressing some words of condolence. Perhaps the clerk lived alone with no one to talk to, and the bright spot of her day was her friend showing up to buy a drink. Who was I to take that away?

I decided to take Dr. Roos' advice. No more *shoulding*. If I was ten minutes late for work I could just stay a little longer, no big deal. "Ladies, talk all you want. I'll just relax and turn on a little music. What a great day!"

Eventually the car in front drove away and I pulled forward, noticing for the first time there was a tiny black sports car behind the bumper of my three-quarter ton truck. Had I not checked my anger, I would have backed into the little car, and right now would be filling out an accident report with a policeman, and worrying how much my insurance would increase when they had to put a new hood on the little car. Thanks, Dr. Roos. As I drove up to the window and ordered my drink, I decided not to say anything to the clerk. Get another conversation going, and the guy behind me might get angry. I just smiled at her as I handed her my money. She refused to take it.

"I'm sorry I kept you waiting," she said. "Needed to share some things with my friend. Thanks for being so nice about it."

"I want to pay for it," I said.

"On the house," she insisted, motioning for me to drive ahead. I wanted to hug her, where a few minutes earlier I was ready to pour my drink down her neck. As I drove back to work I couldn't help but think what a difference *The Osiris Factor* had made in my life this day, and the difference it could make in other people's lives too, especially those who struggled with anger. I knew if this book became a best-seller the world would be a better place for a lot of people.

INTRODUCTION

The recent horrific terrorist attacks on the United States are but the latest example of massive human destructiveness. From the beginning of recorded history, humans have perpetrated abominable atrocities against each other. And with improved technology, fewer people can destroy more fellow humans more quickly than ever before.

We might like to think that such barbaric acts are the product of pure evil, committed by beings that are less than human. Unfortunately, this reassuring myth is unfounded in fact. Members of all races, women and men, adults and children have committed homicide, sometimes on a grand scale. It is not unusual for people who were considered normal by family and friends to unexpectedly kill others, including beloved mates and children, and/or themselves.

Although most of us stop short of brutalizing others, the potential for destructiveness lurks within us all. This inner terrorist, which I call the Osiris Factor, underlies anger, guilt, shame, and depression. It is responsible for most relationship failures, and is the basis of destructiveness toward others and toward the self.

This book is not about terrorism or other extreme forms of human destructiveness. Rather, it deals with the everyday problems of the average person. It explains why most of us are not as happy or fulfilled as we could be. It shows why we often fail to realize our potential as the most extraordinary creations of the known universe, and why we tend to sabotage the achievement of our cherished goals. Although most of us yearn for peace, we are often at war with the persons we love most. Many of us are at war with ourselves.

Overcoming the Osiris Factor will bring you peace—within yourself and with others. By providing practical tools and a new perspective on life, the book will teach you how to recognize and overcome your inner terrorist. It will free you of the negative emotions that sap your time and energy. And it will help you to set goals and make decisions that will foster your emotional and spiritual growth through the coming years.

ONE

THE COMMON ELEMENT

Married to a loving husband, mother of two healthy teenage boys, and successful in her career as a computer programmer, Jill consults me because of recurring anger outbursts and feelings of guilt. Why, like so many people, is she unhappy when things seem to be going well in her life? Tragedy, crisis, or loss may lead to suffering, but often my clients tell me that, although their life is going well, they are nonetheless angry, stressed, guilty, dissatisfied with themselves, unhappy in their relationships, depressed, and so forth. Often they have no idea why they are suffering, although they usually blame events or other people.

On the other hand, many people cope well with adversities. For them, life's challenges and frustrations lead to learning and personal growth. So why, under the same circumstances, do some people benefit, while others plunge into misery and wallow in painful emotions?

Years of working with all kinds of clients as a clinical psychologist have impressed me with the validity of the familiar observation that we are our own worse enemy. Most people are responsible for most of their problems. But they usually do not know how they sabotage themselves. Even when they think they understand why they are troubled, they do not know what to do about it. And when they have sought help from counselors or books, they have often felt overwhelmed by the complexity of the recommended solutions.

I am now convinced that if people would understand and apply *one basic concept* to their lives, they would solve many of their most troublesome, recurring problems. This book presents the concept, which I call the **Osiris Factor**, and shows you how to discover it in your life and how to overcome it. The result will be **freedom from most inappropriate emotions, release from problems of self-esteem and self-confidence, and rewarding relationships**.

Something Is Wrong with the World

After fifteen years as a patrol officer, Jim no longer gets an adrenaline rush as he fingers the cruiser's siren and maneuvers easily around drivers who seem deaf to the siren and blind to the flashing lights. "It's another domestic violence," he tells me with obvious contempt. "But shots have been fired, so I guess we better get there quickly." Since one of my roles is that of police psychologist, I often ride with officers from different departments to stay tuned in to "life on the streets" for police officers.

When we pull into the dingy apartment complex, we both unbuckle our seat belts, a practice used by some officers to allow them to duck quickly in case an irate citizen shoots at them. A small crowd has gathered in front of one of the apartments, watching with mixed emotions as two fire fighters kneel by a fallen man. The scene is bathed in the blinking red, white, and blue lights of emergency vehicles, a patriotic display of the nation's colors. As we step out of the car, a young officer, already on the scene, gives us a quick briefing: "This guy here," he says, pointing at the man on the ground, who is cursing loudly, "says that he came here to get his wife to come home, and to 'take care of business.' Seems she was staying with this other dude who lives in the apartment. When he knocked on the door, he says the guy inside told him to go away, and he told him to come out and be a man. So the guy opens the door and shoots him in the gut and splits."

"Anyone know where the shooter's gone?" Jim asks.

"No. Nobody knows anything," replies the other officer. "But he can't have gone far. He doesn't have a vehicle."

"And what's the wife have to say?"

"Oh, she's crying her eyes out. She claims she loves her husband and just wanted him to pay more attention to her and stop drinking."

"We'll cruise around and see if we can find the guy," Jim says without enthusiasm. "What's the description?"

And so it goes.

* * *

In my therapy office, the distinguished-looking engineer is sobbing. "I can't believe she's left me," he blurts out. "She claims I've been abusing her, but I've never laid a hand on her. I love that woman, and I've done everything that I could to be a good provider. I don't drink or gamble or cheat on her. I just don't understand it!"

"How does she claim that you've been abusing her?" I ask.

"I don't get it. She says that I put her down all the time. That I criticize her. Stuff like that."

"Give me some examples."

"Well, recently she told me that she wanted to go to work. But she doesn't need to do that; I make good money. She needs to stay home and take care of the kids. We've argued about that in the past, but she keeps bringing it up. It's like she doesn't listen to me!"

"And what happened when she last brought it up?"

"Oh, I was tired and just didn't want to go through it all over again. I told her she was acting like a spoiled child who had to have her stupid ice cream cone. And I guess I shouldn't have said it, but I called her stupid."

"And then what happened?"

"Nothing. She just said she wouldn't bring it up again, and she clammed up for the rest of the evening."

And so on.

* * *

"I get so mad!" screams the flushed young woman in my office. "It's so unfair! Why can't my supervisor give me credit for all that hard work I've done on the project? Why does she always have to want more?"

"I understand your frustration," I respond quietly. "What did you do?"

"In the past I would have kept quiet and just stuffed my feelings," she responds, clenching her fists. "But I've been reading some books, and now I know not to do that. So I let her know how mad I was. I told her she was being unfair, and I was sick and tired of it!"

"And what happened then?"

"Well, I sure felt better! But then I began to worry that maybe I shouldn't have said that, because she looked pretty mad herself, and I know she tries to get even."

"Do you think that might be a problem for you?"

"Well, yes, now that I think of it. I might as well kiss that promotion I've been hoping for good-bye."

"Not a good career move?"

"I guess not. Seems I shot myself in the foot. But she shouldn't be criticizing me when I work so hard!"

So my client expressed her feelings, but her career just plummeted into the septic tank.

* * *

Leaning forward in her chair, the middle-aged, conventionally dressed client glares at me and hisses through clenched teeth, "I'm sick and tired of praying without results. I don't ask for much, but apparently it's more than God is willing to give me. Here I've been living a good life, doing everything I'm supposed to do, and all I get is garbage!"

"For instance?" I ask.

"Well, you know about my not getting that job I wanted. And then last week, my miserable car broke down again—now it's the alternator or something like that. Something expensive. And my daughter just got a bad report card. She's always done well, and now she got two C's. And my husband keeps ignoring me. I know we haven't had sex in six weeks or more. Nothing's going right!"

"Even though you think that you're deserving, you're not getting what you're asking from God?"

"Yes! And it's been like that my whole life! It's like no matter what I ask, He isn't going to let me have it!"

And on and on.

Something Is Wrong with Me

"I know that I messed up," explains the neatly dressed executive, leaning back in the leather chair opposite me. "I just didn't try hard enough to be a good father." His eyes mist and a tear begins to course down his left cheek. "I was so busy being a big success that I didn't spend the time I should have with that boy. Now it's too late." He shakes his head and stares at the carpet.

"You're disappointed in yourself?" I ask.

"More than disappointed. I'm disgusted with myself! I failed as a father. When you come right down to it, I haven't really done anything right in this life."

"Nothing?"

"Well, nothing to brag about. I guess I did all right in my job, but that's not really important."

"What else have you done well?"

"Oh, well, my wife's still with me after 23 years. But I doubt that she would be if it weren't for her fear of being on her own."

"I know you love golf. How are you at that game?"

"I get by. But let's face it, after playing all these years I should be a par player, and I sure don't measure up to that."

And so on.

* * *

"I'm just messed up," moans the attractive, stylishly dressed woman in my office.

"How so?" I ask.

"I'm maladjusted and come from a dysfunctional family," she explains. "I never do anything well enough, particularly relationships."

"For instance?"

"Well, I'm in my third marriage, and it won't last at this rate. I'm driving the poor man nuts. I can't help myself from worrying that he'll leave me for another woman, and so I'm constantly questioning him, always suspicious. I know he's tired of it."

"How is it working for you?"

"I'm driving him away, I know. But I just feel so terribly anxious that I'm not good enough for him that I'm constantly asking him for reassurance. Asking him to tell me he loves me. Isn't that stupid?"

"You don't like what you're doing?"

"It's ridiculous! I just can't do relationships. It started in my childhood with poor parenting, I know. In my previous therapy I learned all about that, and I know that I've got a big problem with fear of rejection. I'm just immature and maladjusted." She begins to cry.

And so it goes.

* * *

"I don't have any self-confidence," explains my client as he looks out the window of my office. "I'm so shy that I can't get into a relationship. And when I finally do get a date, I always mess it up."

"Sounds frustrating. How do you mess up your dates?"

"I never know what to say. I'm just a dull person. And I'm not attractive enough to make up for my lack of personality. I know that I should be able to overcome all that, and I really get mad with myself. But it seems that the harder I try, the worse I do."

"So your dates usually don't go the way you would like them to go. What successes have you had?"

"Oh, now and again a woman will seem interested, but it never goes anywhere."

"What happens?"

"Well, after a while I realize that the woman's not really interested in me. So I just give up on the whole thing."

"What do you do, when you give up on the whole thing?"

"I just stop seeing her. I know that's really what she wants."

And on into the septic tank.

What Is It?

These vignettes taken from my practice illustrate how the **Osiris Factor** poisons people's lives. It is the common element in all the above situations. **It is responsible for most anger, guilt, shame, depression, lack of self-confidence, low self-esteem, and relationship disturbances.** It is the primary cause of suicide, which in 1995 was one of the 10 leading causes of death, affecting almost 12 persons per 100,000. It causes most aggression, including violence between intimate partners. Twenty-eight percent of couples reported marital violence in the 1970s and 1980s. The

Department of Justice reported in 1996 that 840,000 women experienced non-lethal violence by an intimate partner in the U.S. Thirty percent of female homicide victims (1300 women) were killed by a boyfriend or husband. Genocide, which has led to the killing of millions, and terrorism, which has recently exploded into the headlines and threatens humans throughout the world, are extreme examples of the operation of the same element. But these statistics only hint at the misery and chaos created by the Osiris Factor.

Osiris was the ancient Egyptian God responsible for judging souls after death. He found them either good or bad, and thereby determined their afterlife. Since that time, judgment has been viewed as a major function of most gods, including most contemporary interpretations of deity. It is an awesome responsibility, allegedly casting human souls into states of unimaginable bliss or suffering.

Most of us have, often unintentionally, usurped this divine function and taken it upon ourselves to judge others, the world, ourselves, and, sometimes, even God. I define the Osiris Factor as the **human tendency to judge others and/or oneself as being wrong, and insisting that others and/or oneself "should" be different**. In our grandiosity, we assume godhood. We believe that *we know what is right* for others and/or for ourselves, and we constantly "should" on others and/or ourselves. This generates and maintains the painful emotions responsible for much of human misery. And since most of us have done this thousands of times, it has become a habit of which we are usually unaware.

Origins of the Osiris Factor

At birth, the human brain is primitive and thinking is rudimentary. As if it were a computer—that is technically incorrect—the primitive brain is programmed with irrational programs. That is, our thinking early in life does not fit reality. It *simplifies* things for us and allows us to make rapid decisions. Its irrational "programs" probably had adaptive value for the human species in the past.

One of the primitive programs of the young child's brain is the either/or/all-or-nothing way of thinking. This makes for quick decisions on whether something is desirable or undesirable, safe or dangerous, and so on, allowing for immediate action. The value of this program is evident in prey animals, who react immediately when they detect a predator. They don't waste time evaluating possibilities or degrees of danger; as soon as they discover the predator, they move!

Another characteristic of the primitive brain is to overgeneralize, so that we can respond to whole classes of things without having to evaluate individual instances. Learning that all large, furry, four-legged animals are dangerous takes less time than learning to make distinctions among dogs, coyotes, wolves, and so forth. And learning to differentiate friendly from unfriendly dogs takes even longer.

So it is only natural that young children classify people as good or bad, right or wrong, heroes or villains. This way of thinking is reinforced by adults, who typically tell the young child repeatedly what is right or wrong, not only for the child, but for other people as well. Often generalizations are provided as guidelines to make decisions easier. It is wrong to lie, to steal, to be lazy, to be selfish, to act unfairly, to be disrespectful, and so on. Strangers are dangerous, criminals are wrong, police are right, and so on. Ethnic, racial, gender and other generalities are popular bases for making good/bad, right/wrong decisions. A person's physical appearance may also be the basis for the right/wrong distinction. In myths, fairy tales, books, movies, TV dramas, and so forth, the good are typically beautiful and the wicked are ugly. Children arc sometimes praised for being beautiful, while being admonished for having "been bad" by being told "that's ugly."

It takes years for the brain to mature enough to think more rationally, which involves estimating degrees and nuances that are more realistic than black/white conclusions. Even adults may have difficulty with the concept that things can be both/and rather than either/or. People are *either* good *or* bad, right *or* wrong, loving *or* hateful, and so on. For many people it is difficult to understand that, for example, one can be *both* loving *and* hateful toward the same person.

Rational thinking is considerably slower than the primitive programs of the infant's brain. Furthermore, the higher brain centers, which are responsible for rational thinking, are more vulnerable to physiological problems than the more primitive centers. Stress, fatigue, toxic conditions, mind-altering drugs, infections, hormonal upheavals, and other chemical imbalances are some of the conditions that may impair rational thinking.

Our earlier, irrational mental programs are not lost but continue to operate throughout our lives, and they can replace or over-ride the rational programs. Hence a person can be very bright and usually think rationally, but at times can lapse into the primitive thinking of a young child

The *Osiris Factor is the product of the primitive brain, based on either/or/all-or-nothing, over generalized thinking.* It has its origin in our neurological development as well as in our early conditioning. Our brain predisposes us to think in terms of simple either/or classifications that tend to be overgeneralized, and we are taught to make distinctions based on the right/wrong model. We grow up being judged by others, and we are taught to judge others as well as ourselves.

Maintenance and Reinforcement of the Osiris Factor

One might think that with brain maturation and increasing experience, we would abandon our early judgmental attitude. Unfortunately, the opposite usually occurs. This is due, in part, to the strengthening of the judgment habit through practice. During each day of a child's life, she may judge others and/or herself hundreds of times. And adults may encourage this habit by repeatedly commenting on what is right or wrong with the child, other people, and the world. Since the strength of habits increases with repetition, the right/wrong habit typically becomes firmly established.

Furthermore, our society reinforces the right/wrong, good/bad habit, starting in childhood and continuing throughout life. Fairy tales, myths, and stories dramatically illustrate the struggle between right and wrong. Children may ask adults as they view a film or listen to a story, "Who are the bad guys?" It is usually easy to determine, because the villains are ugly, deformed, too fat or too thin, or in other obvious ways deviate from the cultural stereotypes of what is beautiful and good.

This theme continues into adult fictional writing, films, TV dramas, and so forth. Characterizations are usually obvious; heroes are right, villains are wrong. Even in the so-called "real" world, the right/wrong model prevails. Wrestling (admittedly more of a fiction these days than a reality) is structured around the good guys valiantly battling the villains. Politicians are often heard proclaiming loudly that they are doing "the right thing," implying that their opponents are, obviously, doing "the wrong thing." Countries justify wars and genocide on the basis that they are doing "the right thing." Their opponents deserve to die and be annihilated because they are "wrong." So millions of adult humans continue to think like young children and to assume that they are God.

Characteristics of the Osiris Factor

Learning a habit takes time and effort. But once established, habits occur quickly, automatically, and without much awareness. And the more firmly established, the more difficult they are to replace. This applies to the Osiris Factor. Established early in life, and reinforced consistently throughout our life, it is a strong habit.

Most people make immediate decisions regarding someone's "wrong" actions, even though they may be unaware of it. A driver cuts them out of traffic, or their spouse says something they do not like, and they are suddenly furious. They may only realize later that they decided that the other person was wrong and "should" not have acted as they did. If asked why the person was "wrong," many people are hard pressed to justify their judgment. As I shall discuss later, these judgments are based on beliefs of which the person may not be aware when making the judgment.

When I have presented these ideas to clients, a common response has been: "That makes sense, but it's going to be very hard to change." How true! Changing any firmly established habit is not easy. And when a habit and its underlying beliefs have become a core part of a personality, the task can be daunting. But it can be done. Habits are learned. And anything that is learned can be unlearned and replaced with something else.

Consequences of the Osiris Factor

The Osiris Factor generates emotions that most of us don't like. Emotions are neither good nor bad, neither right nor wrong. They may be appropriate or inappropriate, but appropriateness is often a matter of opinion. What some people consider an appropriate emotion for a situation, other people may consider inappropriate. Likewise, whether an emotion is healthy or unhealthy is often a matter of opinion. I prefer to think in terms of personal *preferences*: Do you prefer to feel as you do, or would you prefer to feel differently?

Here are the basic presentations of the Osiris Factor, expressed as simple formulas:

- Someone else is *wrong* and *should* act/be different—anger
- I am doing/have done something *wrong* and *should* not be doing/have done it—guilt
- I am (as a person) *wrong* and *should* be different—shame
- Guilt and/or shame—depression

So the results of the Osiris Factor are **anger, guilt, shame, and/or depression**. If you prefer to lessen or eliminate these consequences, read on.

In my experience, most people prefer not to feel the emotions generated by the Osiris Factor. Furthermore, anger, guilt, shame, and depression usually interfere with reaching goals. As will be discussed later, goals give our lives direction, and the Osiris Factor is a serious **obstacle to goal achievement**.

Anger tends to drive people away. Most people don't like being around angry persons, and they particularly don't like being the target of anger. So if you desire intimacy or companionship, anger will interfere with reaching those goals. Anger also tends to beget anger; when you express anger toward someone, that person often responds with anger, leading to escalation of anger and deterioration of communication.

Conflict resolution is virtually impossible if the participants are angry. Anger also interferes with logical thinking and effective action. The angrier you become, the more your thinking becomes childlike and irrational. People often say and do things while angry that they later regret. Physical violence and homicide are extreme examples of anger-generated behavior.

Although some people think that guilt is useful in motivating us to act properly, my experience suggests that the opposite is often the case. The guiltier we feel, the more ineffective we are in changing our behavior. Surprisingly, the behavior about which we feel guilt often escalates, leading to more guilt and a negative vicious cycle.

Addictions are a painful example of how guilt contributes to—rather than reduces—an undesirable behavior. For example, Bill has struggled for years to overcome obesity. He has suffered one diet after another, only to eventually give up in frustration. He might decide to eliminate sweets from his diet, but as he finishes a meal, he has a craving for a desert, which he gulps down guiltily, without even enjoying it. Afterwards, he increases his guilt by berating himself for being "weak-willed" and so forth. The resulting guilt increases his sense of worthlessness and contributes to depression. He then tries to reduce these painful feelings by eating more sweets, generating more guilt, and the vicious cycle escalates.

Shame lowers self-esteem and increases depression. Just like guilt, it interferes with coping. By reducing our effectiveness, shame interferes with goal attainment, including development and maintenance of relationships. If you think of yourself as a total worm, you won't believe that other people may want to be with you; you probably won't want to be with yourself. The resulting lack of achievements and loneliness further reduce self-esteem, again leading to a destructive vicious cycle. Shame does not make us better people; it makes us more miserable and less successful people.

In the next chapter I discuss how the Osiris Factor becomes a pervasive part of most people's lives. Once you understand how your life is tainted by this nasty habit, you can—if you choose—replace it with a more desirable habit.

TWO

LIVING IN TWO UNREAL WORLDS

We most often use the Osiris Factor when we find a discrepancy that we do not like between the two unreal worlds in which we live. Perhaps you still think that you are living in reality, but in this chapter I will show you that none of us lives in reality, and that, surprisingly, there are many "realities."

Fantasy World

All humans begin life in a Fantasy World. It is the world of fairy tales, myths, and fantasies with which we are programmed early in life. It is a simple map of how the world should be. It is in part the product of the primitive part of the brain, which thinks irrationally, but it is also the result of much of the garbage to which we are exposed as children. This is the world as we think it *should be.*

Fantasy World is a simple world of black or white, either/or, good or bad, right or wrong. These clear polarities facilitate choices. In this world, we operate from generalities, which make it easy to reach rapid conclusions. For example, if I believe that everyone should always treat me with respect, any time that anyone does not, I can quickly and easily conclude that he is wrong and should not treat me that way, resulting in immediate anger.

Fantasy World is a world of magic, where we can control events and people with superstitions, incantations, or intense feelings. If we say the right thing, feel the right feelings, do what we "should" do, then things will go our way. If we are "good," then Santa Claus will reward us. If we deeply love someone, they will love us in return. If we try hard, we will succeed. And so forth.

In Fantasy World, no distinction is made between beliefs and facts. The primitive brain, which creates this world, does not know the difference, so that opinions and beliefs are accepted as factual and are not questioned.

If this world were strongly and consistently challenged as we grew from childhood into adulthood, perhaps we would abandon it as nice but unrealistic. As the brain matures, we gain the capacity to think rationally and to recognize the craziness of Fantasy World. But it is not challenged in our culture (and probably most others as well). On the contrary, the early myths are reinforced throughout our life. We are bombarded by songs, books, movies, television shows, advertisements, and so forth with recurring themes from Fantasy World. And so we become increasingly convinced that we know how the world should be; it should conform to our version of Fantasy World. And most of us consider the foundations of our Fantasy World as self-evident facts. *We know the difference between right and wrong*. And if anyone disagrees with us, they are obviously wrong; they "should" accept our version of Fantasy World, and, if they don't, we righteously anger ourselves. Others should also conform to the rules and expectations of our Fantasy World. On the other hand, we should conform to the mandates of our Fantasy World ourselves. And if we don't, we feel guilt and shame.

Suppose, for instance, that in your Fantasy World spouses always treat each other lovingly. You find that, at times, your spouse does not treat you lovingly. But when you point this out to her, she tells you that she doesn't think she should always treat you lovingly, and that, when you behave like an ass, she refuses to treat you lovingly. You might decide that her version of Fantasy World is "wrong," and that she should change both her belief and her behavior. And, bingo, next thing you know, you are angry with your beloved.

Many of our core beliefs are functions of our Fantasy World. And many of our early decisions about how to live life come from these core beliefs. And since most of these beliefs are crazy (that is, irrational and unrealistic), our decisions about how to live life often lead to serious difficulties.

In the next chapter, I will discuss typical Fantasy World Beliefs and show you how to discover them. Then later in the book, I will show you how to challenge them and replace them with more useful beliefs.

Perceived World

While continuing to cling to our Fantasy World, we discover a second world: The world as we experience it. The Perceived World is our version of reality. It is the way we think that the world really is, rather than the way we think it should be.

Our perceptions are distorted interpretations of our experience. They are colored by our beliefs, our past, our expectations, our biases, cultural and group influences, and so forth. Consequently, each of us has our own Perceived World, and there is ample evidence to show that different people often interpret the same event in very different ways. Eye-witness testimony, for example, has been shown to be very unreliable. Recent research has demonstrated a phenomenon labeled "attentional blindness," which occurs in many people when they do not see unexpected objects to which they are not paying attention (Carpenter, 2001). Yet most people believe that their version of the world is reality, and that people who have different perceptions from theirs are clearly mistaken.

Our Perceived World is not only the product of our distorted experiences of the world, it is also the product of our memory. And abundant evidence has shown that memory, like perception, is highly selective, biased, and inaccurate. Most memories are not recordings of past events, as if they were stored videotapes, but are rather re-creations of the past. And these re-creations often change with time, so that our memory of an event as we remember it today may be different from how we remembered the same event a year ago, and we may remember it even more differently six months from now. So when someone's recollection of an event changes with time, it does not necessarily mean that he is lying. Studies have also shown that the degree of confidence a person has in the accuracy of a memory has no relationship to its accuracy. Research has shown, for example, that people can have high confidence in memories of things that never happened, while their confidence in memories of real events may be low.

So what most people think is reality is only their personal, distorted interpretation of experience. That is difficult to accept, and many conflicts center on differences of interpretation of "how things are" or of "what really happened" since we think of our Perceived World as reflecting reality and our interpretations of things as being "true."

Resolving Discrepancies

Certainly life would be much easier and more pleasant if our Fantasy World were real. Things would be the way we think they should be, and we would generally be satisfied. To be sure, we might get bored, since there would be little challenge, and life would be predictable. We don't have to worry about that, however, because our Fantasy World typically is vastly different from our Perceived World. Things are so often not the way we think they should be.

When discrepancies are noted between Fantasy and Perceived Worlds, most people conclude that their Perceived World is *wrong*, and that it should change to fit their Fantasy World. That is, the Osiris Factor operates, and they judge the Perceived World as needing to change to fit their version of how things should be. As noted above, if people decide that someone or something outside themselves is wrong, the "shoulding" generates anger. If they decide that their own behavior is wrong, the "shoulding" generates guilt. If they decide that they, as a person, are wrong, the "shoulding" generates shame. And depression follows guilt and/or shame.

Unfortunately, the Perceived World does not change in response to our "shoulding" upon it. That is primitive magical thinking, which does not work. Typically, when the Perceived World does not change, we intensify our "shoulding," thereby escalating the unpleasant feelings that result from the Osiris Factor.

For example, suppose that in your Fantasy World you can make people feel happy. In your Perceived World, however, you often are frustrated when, in spite of your best efforts, people you care about are not happy. You might then conclude that what you are doing is not good enough, that it must be wrong, since you should succeed in making them happy. This would lead to guilt and reduced self-esteem. You might instead, or in addition, decide that these people should be happy because of your efforts, that they are wrong for remaining unhappy, leading to anger toward them.

The more different your Fantasy World is from your Perceived World, the more you use the Osiris Factor, the more miserable you feel, and the more screwed up your life becomes.

But in spite of massive evidence that neither our Fantasy World nor our Perceived World is an accurate version of reality, we seldom question the validity of either of them.

Being God

Insisting on the "truth" of our beliefs about how the world should be and how the world is makes us a god. We "know" what other people apparently do not know, whenever they disagree with us. Somehow our version of reality is the "right" version. We perceive things accurately; our "truth" is the "real truth." Likewise, our version of how things should be is better than anyone else's version.

And when someone disagrees with us, or does not behave the way we think they should behave, we become righteously angry with them, passing Godlike judgment upon them. We may even try to hurt someone from a sense of righteous vengeance, or in the erroneous belief that we can change the person by punishing him. So we anger ourselves from a sense of grandiosity. We have greater wisdom, understanding, and so forth than those who disagree with us or fail to live life as we think they "should" live it.

Often couples consult me in the hope that I will decide which one of the them is "right" and which one is "wrong." For example, Jim tells me that his wife, Mary, has been staying out late, spending time with her women friends in a bar. "Will you tell her," he asks me, "that what she's doing is bad for our marriage? She needs to spend her evenings with me rather than run around with those women." Jim "knows" what is good or bad for the marriage, and he wants me to agree with him, so that his wife will change her ways and do "the right thing." Mary, on the other hand, also assuming that she has Godlike wisdom, responds heatedly: "Well if he wouldn't neglect me and spend all his time in front of the TV, I wouldn't have to seek companionship with my friends!" And so I am asked to arbitrate disputes between partners, each of whom believes that he is God and "knows" how this partner "needs" to change. Unfortunately, these interactions typically lead to an escalation of anger and alienation between the partners.

Even in those cases where someone decides that she, herself, is wrong, and that she "should" change, there is the assumption that, like God, she has the power and the right to punish "wrong-doers," including herself. So she flagellates herself believing, erroneously, that if she punishes herself severely enough (that is, feels enough guilt), she will change and do what she "should" do and be the kind of person she "should" be.

Paradoxically, even persons with low self-esteem often operate from the Osiris Factor, passing harsh judgment on themselves and/or others. They may not think much of themselves, but they nonetheless make Godlike judgments. These clients may introduce a critical statement about themselves or others by saying "I may not know much, but I do know that..."

Reality

Since our Perceived World is a distortion, what is "reality?" Most people might agree that reality is the world of "facts." It is "objective," whereas perceptions and memories are subjective, according to this view. The problem with this definition lies in defining a "fact." Science discovers facts. By using objective observations and applying the scientific method, scientists strive to eliminate personal bias and the effect of preconceptions. In theory, this is a great approach, but in practice it is becoming increasingly evident that it is virtually impossible to rule out subjectivity. Furthermore, even physicists now recognize that the very process of observing a phenomenon influences that phenomenon, so that discovering truly objective data may be impossible.

The history of science is filled with examples of how "facts" have changed with time. What was once considered factual may later be recognized as inaccurate. For example, we now "know" that the earth is not flat, that it is not the center of the universe, and that the sun, moon, and planets do not circle around it. But in the past, these statements would have been considered serious violations of known "fact," and in some cases could lead to persecution of those who made them. Quantum mechanics and Einstein's principle of relativity have greatly changed the "factual" basis of modern physics. And so on.

So don't be too sure you—or anyone else—can really "know" reality. For practical purposes, I define reality as the consensus about the world of the specific group of which we are members at the time. The reality of the quantum physicist is different from that of the psychologist, which is different from that of the Australian Aborigine, and so forth. So reality changes from time to time and from group to group.

If our Perceived World is vastly different from the reality of the group to which we belong, we will usually be considered "strange," and sometimes "crazy." If, while participating in a conference attended by psychics and mediums, I speak of auras and channeling, the group will listen with understanding and interest. But if I make identical remarks among a group of my psychological colleagues, chances are that many will find validation for their already significant suspicions that I am a "nut case."

In short, none of us has a monopoly on knowing what is real, much less on knowing how things should be. But whenever we operate from the Osiris Factor, we assume that we do have this Godlike knowledge.

Humility

The opposite of grandiosity is humility, the recognition of our limitations. When we become humble, we take a giant step toward overcoming the Osiris Factor. When I accept that my Fantasy World is no better than yours, I will not insist that you are wrong for not complying with my version of how you should live, or for not believing as I do about how things should be. And when I accept that my Perceived World is no more accurate than yours, I will not insist that you change yours to fit with mine. In other words, humility leads me to conclude that I am no more Godlike than other human beings.

Humility is not easily achieved. Children think of themselves as the center of the universe. They are dominated by strong feelings, which determine many of their actions. They want what they want, when they want it, and they believe that they are entitled to it. Repeated frustrations teach them that they do not always have things their way and that they are not the most important thing in the world. Nonetheless, the early sense of omnipotence and entitlement remains a part of all of us. These primitive beliefs can be triggered even in mature adults. Some people never abandon them and continue to live life as if they were entitled to whatever they want and as if their beliefs and opinions were divinely inspired and self-evident truths. When the world frustrates them, they react with anger.

Most people revert to primitive childhood beliefs only occasionally. When dominated by the Osiris Factor, they once again assume they are Godlike and superior to other humans. They "know" how they should be, how others should be, and how the world should be. They also "know" how the world is. And when they note a discrepancy between these two versions of the world, they insist that the world is "wrong" and "should" change. Whenever someone operates from this grandiose, Godlike position, anger, shame, guilt, and/or depression will result.

Humility does not mean assuming a subservient role or discounting our beliefs, opinions, and feelings. Admitting that we are not God does not mean that, therefore, we are ignorant, worthless worms. It means, rather, that we do not delude ourselves into thinking that our Fantasy World is better than that of other people and that our Perceived World is more accurate than that of other people.

THREE

BELIEFS

The Osiris Factor consists of judging ourselves, others, and/or the world based on beliefs about how life should be (Fantasy World) and beliefs about how life is (Perceived World). If humans had the humility to consider that their beliefs are no better or more accurate than the beliefs of others, destructive anger and its horrendous consequences would disappear. Terrorism and genocide would become historical aberrations. But most people are firmly convinced that they know how life should be and how life is. If others disagree, they are wrong. If others do not act the way that they should, they are wrong.

Beliefs and Facts

As previously noted, children don't understand the difference between beliefs and facts. And most adults continue to cling to their core beliefs as if they were facts. Although many of these beliefs are irrational, these people seldom challenge these beliefs (Ellis, 1994,1995). They may even be unaware that they hold them, since these beliefs have become the foundation of their interpretation of the world (Perceived World) and the basis on which they judge the world (does it fit their Fantasy World?).

Beliefs about the world can be right or wrong if they are based on facts that can be verified objectively. For example, if I believe that my car's engine is a V6, I can look at it and count the spark plug wires, which will provide the evidence to prove my belief right or wrong. Likewise, some actions are right, and some actions are wrong—when they pertain to facts. Assume that I intend to drive to Austin and end up in Abilene. Since Abilene is not Austin, I made at least one wrong choice. This conclusion does not involve the Osiris Factor. But if I berate myself for having made the wrong choice and tell myself that I should not have made that mistake, that it reflects something wrong with me, and so forth, I am "shoulding" on myself and generating guilt and /or shame; the Osiris Factor is at work.

So **issues of right or wrong that do not involve value judgments are not expressions of the Osiris Factor**. They do not generate the intense painful emotions produced by the Osiris Factor. If I end up in Abilene instead of Austin, I might be disappointed and frustrated. But I won't be angry ("That should not have happened!"), guilty ("I should not have done that!"), or feel shame ("I'm stupid and need to have my head examined!"), unless I trigger the Osiris Factor and judge the world and/or myself.

Beliefs about how the world should be (Fantasy World) are never right or wrong, since they are value judgments rather than statements of fact. Beliefs about how the world is may be right or wrong or they may be judgments. The belief that a lynx is a member of the cat family can be verified by consulting references or asking biologists; this is a matter of fact, so that the belief can be right or wrong. The belief that all lynx are nasty animals is neither right nor wrong, since it is a matter of opinion. Some people might detest the beasts, some people might cherish them, and some people might like some of the beasts and dislike others.

Fantasy World Beliefs

Beliefs about how the world should be develop early in life and are usually reinforced by our culture on a continuing basis.

These beliefs are often considered to be "self-evident truths," and we may be incensed when someone disagrees with their validity. We often cherish these beliefs, and they can become guiding principles of our lives. Here is a partial list of common Fantasy World beliefs about self, the world, and relationships. They may seem highly desirable, but they are all irrational, since they do not fit reality.

Beliefs About Self:

- I should have total control of my emotions.
- Whatever I do, I should always strive for perfection.
- My self-esteem is based on my achievements.
- My self-esteem is based on my physical attractiveness.
- I need other people's approval to feel good about myself.
- People will reject me if I am flawed or a failure.
- If I am not loved, I am not loveable and/or life is not worth living.
- I should always do my best.
- I can accomplish anything, if I just set my mind to it and want it strongly enough.
- If I keep failing, I should keep trying harder.
- To be a complete human being, I must be deeply involved with at least one significant other.
- I should always strive to improve myself.
- I must meet the needs of others.
- I must take care of others, including their feelings.
- I must meet my own standards in order to be worth-while.
- I should have whatever I really want.
- I must not be prevented from achieving my goals or getting my needs met.
- I must be allowed free expression of my feelings and impulses.

- I know what is best for me, the world, and other people.
- I should not have to deal with unpleasant or scary situations.
- I must rely on someone stronger than myself to deal with life.
- To be worthwhile, I must help others and feel upset over their problems.
- There is always a right solution to my problems, and I must always find that solution.
- It's unacceptable for me to please myself, and I should feel guilty if I do so.
- I should drive myself hard to avoid becoming lazy or irresponsible.
- I should always have high self-confidence.
- I should not have negative thoughts or feelings about people I love.

Beliefs About the World:

- The world should be fair.
- The world should make sense.
- There is only one right solution to every problem.
- Life should be easy.
- It is easier and better to avoid than to face certain life situations and personal challenges.
- The righteous are ultimately rewarded and the wicked punished.
- We are never challenged with more than we can handle.
- There is a good reason for everything that happens.
- Some groups of people (racial, ethnic, national, etc.) are evil and should be destroyed.

Beliefs About Relationships:

- There is a right person for me somewhere in the world, and when I find him/her we'll live happily ever after.
- People who really love each other do so unconditionally.
- My significant other should always treat me with respect and caring.
- People who love each other shouldn't fight.
- People should treat me fairly and with respect.
- People should act the way I want them to act.
- Real friends should always be there for each other.
- To be a complete person, I must be in an intimate, romantic relationship.
- People in an intimate relationship are responsible for each other's feelings.
- Longterm, romantic, intimate relationships should be based on being in love, and if one or both partners fall out of love, there is something wrong with the relationship.
- People who love each other should spend as much time as possible with each other.
- Others should treat me the way I would treat them.
- It is necessary for adults to be cared for, respected, and admired for them to feel good about themselves.
- Other people should not act wrongly, and if they do, they should be blamed, criticized, and punished.
- People should always be honest, and anyone who lies should never be trusted.

Perceived World Beliefs

Beliefs about how the world is are based on opinions of other people, personal experience, and acquired information from many sources, such as books, schools, TV, movies, and so forth. Some of these beliefs are factual and others are not. The irrational beliefs are often overgeneralizations and/or distortions of facts. Most people, unfortunately, fail to distinguish their rational from their irrational beliefs. The irrational beliefs about the Perceived World are generally more individualistic than Fantasy World beliefs, which tend to be widely endorsed by the culture. They often reflect a person's individual experiences. Here are a few examples of irrational beliefs about how the world is:

- I am lacking, and whatever I do is never good enough.
- I am the product of my past and cannot overcome the results of past events in my life.
- I am powerless over addictive cravings, and therefore I am not responsible for addictive behavior.
- I am the victim of genetic and/or chemical problems and therefore am powerless to change.
- Other people or events in my life cause my feelings and emotions, so I have no control of them.
- I have done things that are wrong, therefore I should feel guilty and worthless.
- I have been a bad person, therefore I am worthless and should feel shame.
- People can't really change.
- Certain things in life are awful, and I can't stand them!
- Life is terribly dangerous, and I should constantly worry about potential dangers.
- Life is terrible, hardly worth living, an ordeal, and continuing to face life is a constant pain.
- People are basically nasty and intentionally hurt, abuse, cheat, lie, connive, or take advantage of others.
- We are all governed by fate or some other power so that we have no control over our personal lives.
- People can't be trusted.

- Unless we understand the underlying reasons for our problems, we can't solve them.
- Nothing in life makes sense.

Strengthening Beliefs

Beliefs gain their strength through repetition and reinforcement. This operates differently for Fantasy World beliefs than for Perceived World beliefs.

Fantasy World Beliefs:

The myths, fairy tales, stories, and opinions of people who are important to us form our early beliefs about how the world should be. We accept these beliefs as facts, and they become the basis for which we judge ourselves, the world, and our relationships. They are the foundation of the Osiris Factor. Unfortunately, most of them are irrational, since they do not fit reality. It would be nice if the world were fair, but it often isn't. It would be nice if we could achieve anything we wanted to, but we often can't. It would be nice if someone loved us unconditionally, but most people will put conditions on their love. And so on.

Most of these beliefs are reinforced by our culture, as expressed by common opinion, literature, proverbs, entertainment and news media, advertisements, and so forth. We are continually bombarded with messages that reinforce our irrational beliefs about how things should be. For example, the myth that the righteous will triumph over the wicked underlies much of our fictional writing, TV dramas, movies, and so forth. The belief that physical beauty is a measure of our worth likewise permeates our culture; heroes are beautiful, villains are ugly. Even "self-help" gurus would have us believe that if we only visualize, desire, and work hard enough, we can accomplish anything. People who in some way symbolize popular Fantasy World beliefs (movie stars, successful athletes, financial moguls, and so on) are idolized and held up as models to be emulated.

So rather than abandoning our early irrational beliefs about how things should be, we tend to become increasingly convinced of their validity. Whenever we note a discrepancy between these beliefs and our experience of the world, we tend to conclude that *the world is wrong and should change to fit our Fantasy World*. This is the Osiris Factor at work, with the resulting negative emotions previously discussed. Seldom do we challenge our Fantasy World beliefs. We might, for example, think "Joe is treating me unfairly, and I know that the world is not always fair, but it *should* be!" A more rational statement would be "I believe that Joe is treating me unfairly in this situation. I realize that is my interpretation of his actions and not fact. I would prefer it if he treated me fairly, but in life things often are not fair."

Perceived World Beliefs:

Beliefs about how the world is are the product of (1) what we are told about the world, (2) our experience with the world, (3) our memories, and (4) the effects of our behavior on the world. Let's consider each of these elements.

We are told a great deal about how the world is, and much of it is misinformation. Important adults share with us their own Perceived World during our childhood. They pass on to us their biases, prejudices, distortions, and so forth. They usually present them as facts, and we, as children, consider them to be facts. From an early age, therefore, we filter our experience through the perceptual screen resulting from the beliefs we learn from others.

Other cultural influences further shape our perceptions of the world. Stories, tales, myths, movies, and so forth not only tell us how the world should be (Fantasy World), but they also tell us how the world is. These culturally transmitted beliefs vary from time to time and from culture (and subculture) to culture. Eskimos, for example, perceive many variations of snow that are unrecognized in other cultures. Cultures with strong ethnic or racial prejudices perceive members of certain ethnic or racial groups in derisive ways. During wars, persons defined as the "enemy" are often perceived very differently from the way the same people were perceived prior to the conflict. Years later, they may be perceived differently again.

Our perceptions are subjective and selective. We magnify some aspects of experience and minimize others. And since we can only focus on a fraction of what goes on around us, we ignore many things. Therefore, no two people experience the same situation identically. Studies on the reliability of eyewitness testimony have consistently found that observers of the same event usually report very different accounts (Cade, 1993; Hammond, 1994; Loftus, 1991; Pendergrast, 1995; Yapko, 1994).

As previously noted, memory is likewise selective and subjective. Experiences, biases, suggestions by others, preferences, and so forth greatly influence what and how we remember. Studies have shown that we cannot distinguish memory of actual from imagined past events (Case, 1993; Hammond, 1994; Loftus, 1991; Pendergrast, 1995; Yapko, 1994). Recent investigators have concluded that all memory is a re-creation and not an actual replay of stored information. So there is ample evidence that memory is not an accurate reproduction of the past and can be tainted by many personal factors.

Furthermore, our beliefs about the world influence how we perceive it and how we remember it. We perceive and recall things in a way that reinforces what we already believe about them. Experiences that are inconsistent with our beliefs are usually overlooked, discounted, or distorted in order to be consistent with our beliefs. The same holds for our recollections of experiences that would threaten our beliefs. The result is a vicious cycle in which irrational beliefs reinforce distorted perceptions and memories that then strengthen the beliefs. This may explain why terrorists living in the United States for years may become increasingly convinced of the wrongness of our country; they only focus on the aspects of the culture of which they strongly disapprove (such as pornography or prostitution) and completely ignore those aspects of the culture that is inconsistent with their belief that the United States is evil, immoral, and so forth.

Our Perceived World is further reinforced by our tendency to behave in ways that will confirm our beliefs. Often we generate what we expect, a form of self-fulfilling prophecy. We are usually unaware of provoking expected situations, and, when they occur, we use them to confirm our beliefs about the world. We do not acknowledge our role in behaving in ways that are likely to produce the expected outcome.

For example, Darla believes that she is unlovable and that no man will stay with her. As her relationship with a desirable man unfolds, she gradually becomes nastier with him, criticizing him and accusing him of not loving her. Eventually, he tires of her nastiness and leaves. She then uses this experience as further evidence of her belief that she is unlovable and that no man will stay with her.

My experience with cats illustrates how beliefs shaped a part of my Perceived World. From my earliest childhood, my parents told me that cats were nasty, deceitful, cruel, and manipulative animals. Accepting this view of cats as fact, I noticed many instances that confirmed their negative attributes. I was alert to them hissing, glaring at me, clawing, chasing mice, killing birds, and so forth. Occasionally, one of the adults in my world might even read me a story of a cat committing a felony. Naturally I was careful to avoid these animals. When confronted by one, I would yell at it, kick at it, throw something at it, and so on, leading to the expected response of hissing and/or galloping away from me. This further convinced me of their inability to form a bond with a human being (namely, me). If a cat approached me in what appeared to be a friendly manner (purring, trying to rub against my legs, and so forth), I was not deceived by the beast's obvious attempts at manipulation and seduction and would kick at it. It would then reveal its "true nature" by hissing at me. As I grew older, I accumulated a rich collection of bad memories about cats. If someone pointed out a cat being affectionate or showed me a news story of a heroic cat, I dismissed these instances as fantasy or as examples of the animal's skill at conning people.

Imagine my consternation when, some 15 years ago, my wife suggested that we invite a cat to join our household. As I presented her with the "facts" about cats which I had wisely accumulated over a lifetime, I suddenly realized that these were beliefs and opinions, not facts. Harnessing my scientific training, I agreed to participate in an "objective" experiment: we would invite a kitten into our home, treat it without negative preconceptions, and note the result. As the saying goes, the rest is history. I am now a committed cat lover and spend many happy hours with these wonderful companions.

Discovering Troublesome Beliefs

Since irrational beliefs are the basis of the Osiris Factor judgments, which lead to negative emotions and actions, you might consider your most troublesome beliefs so that you can, if you wish, replace them. Keep in mind that some of these beliefs refer to the Fantasy World (how you think things should be) and some refer to the Perceived World (how you think things are).

Begin by reviewing the list of irrational beliefs presented earlier in this chapter. Identify those with which you agree, ranking each from one (agree slightly) to five (agree strongly). Then add other beliefs about how things should be (for you, relationships, and the world in general) and how you think they are. Compare these beliefs to the same ranking system. The beliefs ranked four or five are probably causing you the most difficulty. Pay particular attention to any belief that you consider self-evident, obviously true, or a fact of life. These beliefs are probably most troublesome for you.

If you feel angry because I am suggesting a belief is irrational, that belief may be particularly important to you. To check this out, consider how often you get upset because of the belief. For example, suppose one of your strong beliefs is that people should treat you with respect. How often do you get upset by judging people as wrong for not treating you with you respect?

Irrational beliefs can often be identified by words that seldom apply to reality. Words such as "should," "must," "ought," and so on often appear in Fantasy World beliefs. This is the case with statements implying a value judgment, such as "People should tell the truth," or "I must always do my best." When these words refer to factual matters rather than to judgments, they are not signs of irrationality. Examples would be statements such as: "If you want to get to Austin from here, you should go south," or "If you want to stop the car quickly, you must apply the brakes." Other words suggesting irrationality imply overgeneralization. Examples are "always," "everyone," "never/always," "every time," and so on. These words often occur in Perceived World beliefs. Examples would be statements such as "I never satisfy you," or "No one cares about me."

You can further test beliefs for irrationality by subjecting them to the following questions (adapted from Max Maultsby, 1984):

- Is the belief **factual**? Is it consistent with the way things really are rather than with the way you would like them to be (Fantasy World beliefs)? Is it consistent with the way most other people from your culture/group interpret reality (Perceived World beliefs)?
- Will the belief help you to **reach your goals**? For example, if your goal is to feel good, then unrealistic beliefs about how the world "should" be will work against the goal by generating anger, guilt, shame, and/or depression. Likewise, if your goal is intimacy, the belief that "You can't trust anybody" will sabotage the achievement of that goal.
- Will the belief help you to **protect yourself**? Beliefs such as "I must please everybody," or "I must be in a committed relationship to be a complete human being" increase your vulnerability.
- Will the belief help you to keep **out of trouble with other people**? Beliefs such as "Everyone must treat me fairly," or "I must always stand up for what I know is right" may increase confrontations with others.
- Will the belief help you to **feel the emotions you prefer to feel**? Many beliefs, as already discussed, lead to the Osiris Factor with its resulting anger, guilt, shame, and/or depression. Most people would prefer to feel differently.

Let's apply these principles to a sample belief: "People should always be honest." Notice the belief contains two words that suggest problems. "Always" suggests that the belief is an overgeneralization and hence does not fit reality. "Should" suggests that the belief is a fantasy of how we would like things to be rather than a realistic statement of how things are. Let's now apply the five qualifying questions discussed above:

- Is this belief factual? It is not. Many people occasionally lie to some extent. Few, if any, people are 100% truthful always. Indeed, lying is so universal that some psychological tests include statements about total honesty as a measure of "faking," which contributes to the test's validity scales.
- Will this belief help you to achieve your goals? Perhaps it will at times, but at other times it may undermine your goals. Suppose that your boss asks what you think of his latest brainstorm, and you respond with total honesty: "Your idea is not only preposterous but suggests pre-senile dementia." Your goals of promotion and long job tenure are likely to be seriously jeopardized. Or imagine that your goal is to have a close, loving relationship with your mate. Early one morning, as she awakens, she asks you: "Honey, how do I look today?" Since she looks like something that your favorite feline might have drug in during the night, and since you are committed to total honesty, you share this candid observation with her. Chances are that your goal of a close, loving relationship is receding rapidly.
- Will this belief help you to protect yourself? In some situations, unfortunately, lying may save you a job, a relationship, a severe beating, a prison term, and so on. Furthermore, if you believe that everyone should always be honest, you are setting yourself up for much disappointment and pain.
- Will this belief help you keep out of trouble with others?

As already noted, the belief may get you *into* serious trouble.

- Will this belief help you to feel the way you want to feel? If you believe that other people should always tell you the truth and you find them lying to you, the result will be anger. If you lie, you will probably criticize yourself, leading to guilt and loss of self-esteem. If you are like most "normal" people, you would prefer to not feel angry or guilty, and you would prefer to not lose self-esteem.

Notice that Fantasy World beliefs are usually irrational in that they state how things should or must be. There is nothing wrong in having beliefs about how we would **like** things to be. But when we insist that our preference is the "right" belief, and that therefore things "should" conform with our preference, we are assuming godhood and applying the Osiris Factor.

Recognizing irrational beliefs about how things *are* may be more difficult. By accepting that your interpretation of reality is probably no better than other people's, you are less likely to insist that your perceptions and memories are "truer" than other people's. You can validate many Perceived World beliefs by either checking them out with other people, obtaining factual information from recognized references, and/or conducting objective experiments (as I did with cats).

Constructing New Beliefs

Since most of our irrational beliefs were learned long ago and repeated countless times, it will take time and effort to replace them with new beliefs. Below are some basic steps you can take to **replace irrational beliefs** with more useful beliefs. (Be aware that although your new beliefs make sense logically, they won't feel right at first).

▪ *Identify the irrational belief.* As already noted, this often requires detective work, discovering when your feelings are inappropriate or when you are blocking yourself from reaching your goals. Often, noticing when you use the Osiris Factor will reveal Fantasy World beliefs as the bases for your judgments that you or someone else is wrong. Use the guidelines presented earlier in this chapter to ferret out irrational beliefs about your Fantasy World and about your Perceived World.

▪ *Write down the irrational belief.* Be honest with yourself. Write it down, even if you realize that it is crazy or, at least, irrational.

▪ *Develop the new belief.* Take your time so that the new belief will meet the following requirements: It will be **factual**; it will help you to meet your **goals**; it will help you to **protect** yourself; it will help you in your **relationships**; and it will help you to feel the way you want to **feel**. Check it for the words listed earlier as characteristic of Fantasy World beliefs and of irrational Perceived World beliefs. Check out the new belief with a wise friend or counselor, to avoid the possibility of developing another irrational belief. Notice that Fantasy World beliefs remain irrational unless they are reworded as your preferences rather than as imperatives about how things should be. For example, you might replace "People should be honest" with "I prefer to deal with people who are usually honest with me about important matters."

▪ *Write down the new belief.* Getting it on paper makes it more real and allows you to refine it. Writing it on several 3X5" cards allows you to place the cards in strategic spots where you will see them frequently throughout the day.

▪ *Repeat the new belief frequently.* Every time you see one of your strategically placed cards, read the belief to yourself. Use as much conviction as possible, reminding yourself of the evidence for the validity of the belief.

- *Repeat the new belief whenever the old irrational belief is triggered.* With practice, you will more quickly recognize old beliefs. Usually, their impact will be evident in familiar inappropriate feelings or recurring blocks to reaching your goals. As soon as you identify the old belief, challenge it. Then replace it with the new belief. Remember to congratulate yourself for this neat bit of self-reprogramming!

Besides these basic steps, you might add some optional techniques. Since relinquishing an old belief is often a painful loss, expect some grief. Therefore, you might do a *symbolic ritual,* in which you bid the old belief *good-bye.* You might also welcome the new belief with a symbolic ceremony. If the old belief is closely associated with an important person from your past or present, you might have an imaginary conversation with that person. You could, for instance, return the belief to him.

FOUR

MENTAL MOVIES

Previous chapters have shown how the Osiris Factor involves habits of thinking (right/wrong leading to "shoulding") and irrational beliefs (about Fantasy World and Perceived World). This chapter discusses the third aspect of the Osiris Factor: movies or trances.

Beliefs and Movies

We can shift our attention from the world around us to an inner world. We do this when we dream, for example, and create a private world that is inaccessible to others. We can also withdraw into this private world when we are awake and shift our attention inwardly. This is called fantasy, daydreaming, or trance.

We may continue to be aware of the external world—as often happens while driving a car and daydreaming—or we may lose contact with the outside world—as happens when we fail to hear someone question us while we are in a trance. There are degrees of trance, and people differ in their ability and interest in this activity. Probably everyone does it to some degree. Studies have suggested that the average person tends to cycle into a spontaneous trance-like state about every 90 minutes throughout the day. This is probably the same cycle that dominates the sleep patterns, which also occur about every 90 minutes.

During trances, we typically attend to internal images and/or sounds. It is as though we were viewing a film or a TV program. Sometimes, it may be more like listening to a radio, since we may imagine sounds without visual images, such as voices or songs. These experiences are not hallucinations, since we know that we create them. In dreams and hallucinations, we usually interpret the experiences as being real. In some dreams and hallucinations, we may be aware of the unreality of the experiences, but we do not feel in control of them; they seem to happen to us rather than be created by us.

The themes of our trances relate to our beliefs. We tend to select inner movies that confirm our beliefs about how things should be and about how things are. Many of these inner movies are replays of the past that reinforce some of our favorite beliefs. For example, Catherine, who believes that she should be perfect (Fantasy World) and that she "never" does things well enough (Perceived World) selects from an extensive collection of mental movies of past failures and shortcomings. Each time she views one of these movies, she strengthens her beliefs and thus experiences loss of self-esteem and depression.

When viewing inner movies, our feelings are appropriate to the movies rather than to current reality. So Catherine's depression may have nothing to do with what is currently happening to her. She may, indeed, be unaware of what is happening to her because of her focus on her trance experience.

We are not limited to historical movies. Instead of replaying our version of past happenings, we can creatively develop movies about things that *could* happen. For example, Greg keeps himself angry with his boss by creating movies of imagined situations in which his boss berates him, treats him unfairly, and ultimately fires him. Movies of negative future experiences often generate self-fulfilling prophesies since we tend to behave so as to produce what we anticipate. As the result of anger generated by his application of the Osiris Factor (beliefs, shoulding, and movies), Greg acts belligerently and provocatively toward his boss until—surprise—his boss finally does criticize him and fire him. Now Greg feels vindicated, telling himself that he always knew his boss was unfair and would ultimately persecute him.

As the director of our inner movies, we magnify those elements that reinforce our beliefs and minimize or eliminate those elements that are inconsistent with our beliefs. We make no subtle characterizations in our movies; people are good or bad, right or wrong, heroes or villains.

Movies and the Osiris Factor

Past experiences that trigger the Osiris Factor are often replayed in trance. The emotions originally associated with the experiences are then rekindled. In addition, we tend to generate more bad feelings by re-deciding that what happened was wrong and should have been different. We apply the Osiris Factor to the past situation, adding to the unpleasant feelings already associated with it.

It is not that we are full of negative feelings from past situations. Rather, we keep re-generating the feelings whenever we review the memories of the situations. These reviews can occur anytime, but they are most likely to occur when we are dealing with a current situation that is similar in some respect to the old one. We decide that what's happening now is wrong, and we then justify our conclusion by reviewing past examples of similar wrongdoings, thereby justifying and increasing our negative feelings. I think people are mistaken when they say "I have a lot of anger." A more accurate statement would be "I create a lot of anger."

Suppose, for example, that Myrna's sister refuses to babysit for her. Myrna immediately decides her sister is wrong for refusing her request and that she should not have done so. She then reviews movies of past situations in which her sister refused what Myrna thought were appropriate requests. As she rapidly reviews each of these movies, Myrna recalls her anger at the time and adds to it by re-deciding how wrongly her sister acted. She may further intensify these feelings by concluding that her sister is selfish (or insensitive, or stubborn, etc.) and thereby is wrong as a person. Myrna selects only mental movies that support her negative judgment of her sister. If she has collected movies in which her sister was responsive to her requests, she does not review them. And she may never have collected such movies, discounting or ignoring her sister's behavior when it was not consistent with her belief that her sister is "selfish."

In the following example, depression rather than anger is reinforced by a trance. Bill's mother, concerned about his inactivity, says to him: "Bill, don't be so lazy. You need to get out of this house and socialize." Bill triggers the Osiris Factor and immediately concludes that he is wrong for being inactive (guilt) and a poor excuse as a human being for being lazy (shame). He then reviews movies of earlier situations in which he concluded that he was lazy. For good measure, he adds a favorite movie of a situation at age seven when his grandmother told him: "Bill, you'll never amount to anything. You just don't seem to care about anything." This movie reinforces his belief that he is a flawed person, doomed to failure. The results of these trances are guilt, shame, and depression. This was not the intent of Bill's mother, who wanted to counter his depression by getting him involved with people. Unfortunately, by judging him negatively (he's lazy and "needs to...") she has triggered his Osiris Factor.

Selecting Movies

When you go to a multi-screen theater, you select a movie that will help you to feel what you want to feel. If you want to cry and feel sad, you will select a "tearjerker." If you want to laugh, you will go to a comedy. Likewise, you can select the internal movies you view in trance. If you want to intensify anger, guilt, shame, and/or depression generated by the Osiris Factor, you will choose to select movies that will reinforce your negative judgment of self (for guilt, shame, and depression) or of others (for anger).

On the other hand, if you prefer to reduce the feelings generated by the Osiris Factor, select movies that will invalidate your negative judgments. Suppose that you have just completed an abominable game of golf, and you tell yourself: "I really screwed that up! Once again, I didn't do it well enough. The harder I try, the worse I get. I keep failing, and I guess that I'm just a failure!" This internal expression of the Osiris Factor generates shame ("I'm a failure") and contributes to depression. If you now select movies of past successes on the golf course, as well as in other aspects of life, the absurdity of your conclusion that you are a "failure" will become obvious. Furthermore, you will re-experience some of the positive feelings you had with your past successes.

Unfortunately, people who specialize in anger have impressive movie collections of examples of other people's wrongdoings and few—if any—movies of being treated well by others. People who specialize in depression, on the other hand, have massive movie collections of personal inadequacies and misdeeds and few—if any—movies of personal successes and validation by other people. It may be difficult, therefore, for such people to select positive movies, since they may not have collected them.

Here is how you can use your trances to counteract the Osiris Factor:

- Identify movies in your internal collection that invalidate your negative beliefs about yourself and other people.
- Create new movies based on re-interpretation of past events and on current experiences that invalidate your negative beliefs about yourself and other people.
- Catch yourself whenever you are viewing a movie that reinforces the Osiris Factor ("I was wrong" and/or someone else was wrong).
- Immediately shift to one of the positive movies that you now have handy for the occasion.
- Congratulate yourself on recognizing and countering the Osiris Factor, and remind yourself that you are not God and that's all right!

Out of the Theater

You might prefer to come out of trance when you find yourself in a bad internal movie. While most people can't come out of dreams at will, they can learn to come out of waking trances. The key element is to shift focus of attention from your internal to your external experience. This requires shifting from fantasy to reality (or, more accurately, your perception of reality). Once you have exited the inner theater of your mind, you can respond to the current situation without accessing the Osiris Factor. Your feelings will then be appropriate to the situation.

Here are the steps you can take to exit the theater and come out of trance:

- Recognize that you are in trance and focused within yourself rather than attending to the external situation.

- Congratulate yourself on your discovery.
- Focus your attention on your environment, actively attending to details (colors, shapes, sounds, temperature, and so on).
- Keep shifting your attention to different aspects of the environment.
- Actively interact with the environment, by moving about, talking, engaging in a compelling activity, and so forth.

FIVE

GOALS

We have seen how we generate anger, guilt, shame and depression by assuming that our interpretation of how things should be and how they are is *the* right version. Irrational beliefs, habits of right/wrong thinking, and mental "movies" reinforce each other to activate and maintain the Osiris Factor and its negative consequences.

But if we are to abandon this familiar approach to life, what are we going to substitute for it? As one of my distraught clients recently stated, "I've always thought this way. And I don't know what else to do!" She then began sobbing painfully as she contemplated relinquishing some of her cherished beliefs and her automatic response to conflict with others and herself (blame someone).

Part of the answer to this question is to replace making judgments about right and wrong with determining what **works and what does not work in helping us to reach our goals**. If our actions move us toward our goals, they are working, and we can continue our progress by doing more of the same. If our actions interfere with reaching our goals or move us no closer to them, then they are not working, and it would be wise to experiment with doing something different. This approach not only helps us to reach our goals, but it produces valuable **learning**, which, in turn, leads to increased **wisdom**. This requires us to have useful goals. This chapter shows you how to develop and reach such goals.

Most people live their lives without goals. When pressed, they may mumble something about "being happy," "feeling self-fulfilled," "living a good life," or other equally vague, intangible and unrealistic ideas. These types of goals are useless. You will never know if you reach them. And your chances of reaching them are virtually nil. So they provide you no guidance for action, and you won't know if what you are doing is working or not.

Useful Goals

I define a goal as a *desired condition that provides an incentive to action*. Unless a goal **motivates you to act**, it's pointless—an exercise in futility. This mean that at least a part of you wants to achieve the goal and is willing to work for it. So the first quality of a useful goal is that it is something that you ***really want.***

Some people seek goals that they think they *should* or *need* to reach. Forget that. People seldom reach their "should" goals, unless at least a part of them also wants to reach the goal. When you choose a goal, be sure that you want it, that it is important to you.

It is equally essential to select **realistic** goals; that is, goals that you can reach with reasonable effort. A popular Fantasy World belief is that "We can accomplish anything if we just try hard enough" or "if we just want it badly enough." Unfortunately, these beliefs can be found in some self-help literature. But none of us can accomplish everything we might desire. We all have limitations. And accepting them lets us focus our time and energy on activities that have a reasonable chance of success.

In my youth, I aspired to become a professional singer. I studied voice, listened to successful singers, practiced diligently, visualized myself singing in front of cheering crowds, and so forth. Unfortunately, I happen to be almost totally tone deaf. Too bad, so sad, and so on. For that reason, becoming a professional singer was an unrealistic goal for me. And when I finally accepted that bit of bad news, I replaced that goal with more realistic ones. As a result, I channeled my time and energy into successfully pursuing other more realistic goals.

On the other hand, avoid goals that are too easily met. For a goal to be motivating, it must be **difficult enough to be challenging**. If a goal is not challenging, reaching it will not provide a sense of satisfaction. To be sure, some goals are not very challenging and yet they may be important. For instance, my daily goal of getting out of bed each morning is not always a major challenge (although I find it becoming more challenging by the day). But it is necessary to reach other goals. So this goal may be important, but it is not highly motivating. On getting out of bed each morning, I only give myself a soft pat on the back. I do not celebrate this daily event as a major victory or a brilliant accomplishment.

The fourth characteristic of a useful goal is that it is **tangible**. That is, it can be seen, touched, measured, or otherwise recognized objectively. Unless a goal is tangible, you have no way of knowing whether you have reached it. You don't know how successful your actions are in making progress toward it. Consequently, it is useless. Choosing unmeasurable goals gives people the most trouble.

Take, for example, the goal of no longer being sad. Since most people think of sadness as a feeling, they find that it changes from day to day and from moment to moment. Furthermore, it may be influenced by events over which they have little or no control. Therefore, they may be frustrated when they conclude that they are failing to reach their goal. This may intensify their sadness, since they may blame themselves for not doing the "right thing." And self- blame generates and increases depression.

More tangible goals related to sadness might include "initiating at least five contacts with other people during each of the next five days," or "identifying at least 10 daily accomplishments at the end of each day for the next week," or "staying out of the house at least four hours a day for the next three days," etc. You can determine how well you meet each of these goals. And the degree to which you meet them will influence your sadness.

You can determine if a goal is tangible by asking yourself "How will I know when I have reached this goal?" If you can't answer this question, the goal is probably intangible. Don't settle for answers such as "I'll just know," or "I'll feel different." Feeling goals are usually intangible, and therefore of little value, and your assessment of how you feel is, at best, subjective.

If you insist on feeling goals, such as "I'll stop feeling depressed," use numerical ratings to quantify your feelings. Percentages work well. You might, for example, rate your average daily depression each evening, expressed as a percentage. You might then find that, over several weeks, your daily average rating has decreased from 75% to 54%. If your goal had been total freedom from depression, you might interpret this finding as failure. You might then use this conclusion to depress yourself further by overgeneralizing and judging yourself negatively ("I always fail," and "I am a failure."). On the other hand, if you think of feelings as having degrees, you might think of reducing depression from 75% to 54% as evidence of progress.

One reason that feeling goals are often not useful is this tendency to think in all-or-nothing terms. Setting a goal of totally eliminating a feeling is unrealistic. No matter how rational we are, or how much we practice rational habits of thinking, negative feelings are liable to surface occasionally. When they do, it is best to accept them without self-judgment.

You can also decide whether a goal is tangible by asking, "How will other people know when I have achieved this goal?" Usually, if others can't identify when you've reached a goal, it is intangible. Feeling goals usually fall in this category, since others can't know how you feel. They can, on the other hand, know whether you call them on the phone at least once a week, or give them at least one compliment a day, or spend at least 15 minutes a day with them. Since other people can observe these goals, they are tangible.

Useful goals are also **consistent with our values**. If a goal violates an important value, it will generate internal conflict. When a goal violates one of our basic values, we may try to justify it with rationalizations. Or we may try to deceive ourselves by disguising the goal to make it seem to fit our values.

Suppose, for example, that I set as a goal making as much money as possible by swindling gullible people. This goal might conflict with one of my values, such as treating others as I would like them to treat me. I might try to rationalize this goal by telling myself: "If I don't do it, someone else will," or "If they're that stupid, they deserve to be duped," and so on. Or I might try to convince myself that the people I swindle are really benefiting, since I am teaching them a useful lesson; therefore, I am really doing them a favor.

The problem with trying to con ourselves about goals that violate our values is that we usually know, at a deep level, what we are doing. And we don't feel good about it. Our sense of self, our identity, is threatened. And we are prone to develop guilt and/or to sabotage ourselves.

Obstacles

As you develop goals, you may already be anticipating obstacles that will get in your way. Often, the same obstacles have prevented you from reaching goals in the past.

By identifying the obstacles that may prevent you from reaching a goal, you can prepare to overcome them. Unless you deal with obstacles in your goal-setting, you will probably continue to fail to reach your goals.

Obstacles can be either external or internal. **External obstacles** are situations, conditions, or people other than yourself. For example, lousy weather may sabotage your goal of playing golf. Or your goal of spending one hour per night studying the language of the Australian Aborigines may be jeopardized by your husband's insistence that you spend every waking moment talking with him. Don't underestimate the importance of external obstacles. Some people discount their importance. They may tell themselves, "I'll deal with that when it happens," or "Where there's a will there's a way." Such nice-sounding intentions seldom overcome the obstacles. Then when they occur, the goal may be lost.

Internal obstacles are often more difficult to identify than external ones. The old saying that we are our own worst enemy often applies to reaching goals. We are not a unified entity. Rather, as will be discussed in a later chapter, we have different parts, which often have different beliefs, feelings, attitudes, and goals. Consequently, we can be buffeted by internal conflicts that can sabotage our efforts to reach our goals.

You can identify internal obstacles by reviewing what happened in the past when you failed to reach a goal since you are likely to repeat the same mistakes. You can also identify potential internal obstacles by asking yourself if any part of you objects to the goal. You might ask yourself, "Will any part of me be unhappy or frustrated if I reach this goal?" Then accept whatever answer you get, seriously and with respect, and note it as an internal obstacle.

Here's an example of internal obstacles to reaching a goal. A bright, motivated woman recently consulted me to help her lose weight and retain the weight loss. In the past, she had often lost much weight, using popular weight loss programs. Unfortunately, she had always regained the weight (and then some) shortly after completing her weight loss goal.

I asked her to get in touch with any part of her that objected to the goal. She became aware that part of her feared being approached by men. And that part believed that the extra weight kept men away. However, this belief was only partly valid, since the weight only restricted the quantity and quality of men approaching her. She also became aware of another part of her that objected to becoming thin. This part believed that losing weight would satisfy her mother. And she didn't want to do that. For years her mother had insisted that my client should lose weight. And, of course, my client did not want her mother to get credit for the weight loss. Regaining weight was a way of triumphing over mother.

Overcoming Obstacles

Once you have discovered obstacles, develop **action plans** for overcoming them or minimizing their effect. Avoid the old Fantasy World beliefs that trying hard will lead to success, or that wanting something badly enough will get it. Those are irrational beliefs, which have no foundation in fact.

You can often overcome external obstacles with straightforward actions. The specific actions will depend on the nature of the obstacle. They might be as simple as avoiding certain places and people (as when your goal is to overcome an addiction). For example, if your goal is to lose weight, you might avoid some types of restaurants and stores. Avoiding certain people can be as simple as refusing invitations from specific individuals, or it can be as complicated as divorce.

Actions might include negotiating acceptable compromises

with other people. Consider the previous example of a husband who insists that his wife spend every waking moment talking with him. She might get his agreement that she will spend one hour each evening with him. Or he might consent that she studies her language materials while he sits quietly in the same room, and so forth.

Nevertheless, there may be times when you will be unable to overcome external obstacles through action. For example, you may find that your job is a major obstacle to reaching one of your goals. However, leaving the job may not be a valid option at this time. In such cases, you may have to modify your reaction to the obstacle to achieve your goal. Often, the reason that something becomes an obstacle is that we upset ourselves about it. It may not be the event or situation that prevents us from reaching our goal, but rather the fact that we become highly upset about the event. In the above example, it may not be the job itself that prevents you from reaching your goal. The negative feelings you generate about the job, on the other hand, can become serious obstacles.

Here's an example of this last point. I recently saw a young married couple in which the wife complained that her husband was "unfit to live with." She described his constant moodiness and nastiness. The husband admitted to being moody and hard to get along with. But he justified this behavior by explaining that his job was so frustrating, it "made" him mad. When he came home he had to "get the feelings out." Although his goal was to be kind and charming with his wife, he said his job kept him from reaching this goal. He had considered changing jobs, but he was unwilling to do so at that time, due to income, benefits, seniority, etc.

To overcome this obstacle, this man needs to change his reaction to his job. He also needs to stop angering himself about it. He can accomplish this by accepting his job as it is, rather than insisting that it should be different, and that it is wrong for being the way it is. In this way he can work to overcome the Osiris Factor.

Another option might be to modify his behavior while continuing to generate anger and upset. He could, for example, discharge his anger when reaching home by exercising vigorously. He could then tell himself that he doesn't need to think about the job again until he returns to it the following day. He might then treat his wife lovingly and charmingly and reach his goal.

To summarize, you can overcome external obstacles by **acting appropriately**, by modifying the feelings about the obstacles, and/or by **acting differently in response to the feelings.**

Overcoming internal obstacles can be more challenging. As noted above, identifying internal obstacles often requires detective work. They are sometimes the result of parts of us that operate outside our awareness. To discover these parts, we must accept the fact that we can want opposite things simultaneously, although this may seem illogical. For example, we can both want to lose weight and want to remain overweight. We may want to succeed and we may want to fail.

Resolving internal conflict is discussed in greater detail in chapter 9, but here is a summary of how to deal with internal obstacles. Having **identified internal objections** to achieving a goal, the next step is to **accept** each objection without criticism or upset. Then learn the **intention** of each objecting part. Discover what each wants to accomplish for you. All our internal parts are usually positively intentioned, although the resulting behavior may undermine our goals. Since some of our parts are remnants of our childhood and think illogically, their positive intention may be based on magic or other forms of irrational thinking.

Consider, for example, a suicidal woman I recently interviewed. When I questioned the part responsible for her suicidal ideas, I learned that its intention was to reduce the woman's intense emotional pain. This part believed that the only escape from this pain was through death.

Once you have identified a positive intention by the part objecting to your goal, **validate** that intention. In the above example, most people would agree that reducing emotional pain is a valid goal. When you have identified and validated each part's intention, express your **appreciation** to the part. By appreciating those parts that object to your goal, you make friends of them rather than enemies. This sets the stage for **negotiating** among your various parts so that they can reach agreement regarding goals. Only when all your parts subscribe to your goals will you reach these goals without internal self-sabotage.

Magic

Reaching goals often requires hard work and time. But parts of us are typically impatient and lazy. They want immediate results without effort. So they may object to working toward a goal, even though they do not object to the goal itself. For example, in setting the writing of this book as a goal, I found none of my parts objected. When it came to doing the work, however, it was a different matter. Frequently, I had difficulty getting the job done. One or more of my immature parts would often rebel at the effort and time required by the task.

A favorite strategy of our primitive parts is to resort to **magic**. Instead of doing the tedious work of writing a book, for example, these parts much prefer to fantasize about achieving the goal. They like daydreaming and talking about hard work much more than they like doing it. Furthermore, popular Fantasy World beliefs reinforce magical thinking. "If I want something strongly enough, I will get it" is one of these irrational beliefs. A related belief, popular with "Positive Mental Attitude" gurus, is that positive affirmations will achieve our goals. For example, if I tell myself often enough, with enough conviction, that "I will complete an outstanding book," it won't be long before the completed book appears on the Bestseller list.

Similar magical thinking underlies beliefs that a force or power outside our self ("Higher Power," "God," "Cosmic Mind," and so forth) will achieve our goals for us. Magical rituals, incantations, prayers, and such may be used to invoke the good graces of whatever force we think will bring us success.

Another common belief is that clearly visualizing the achievement of a goal will (magically) realize the goal. So if I were to repeatedly visualize the name of this book on a Bestseller list, eventually the book would be a Bestseller.

To be sure, this magical thinking is delightful, and worthy of anyone's Fantasy World, but there is a major problem with it: It does not work, because it is irrational and unrealistic. There is no substitute for doing the work to achieve a goal. And believing that we can achieve it through magic will sabotage reaching it.

Although irrational, for many people these magical beliefs and practices can be useful. They might increase motivation, self-confidence, and so forth. But they are not substitutes for the work required to reach a goal. Though we might prefer not working hard, most worthwhile goals will require us to do so. Magical approaches may make things easier, but they will not get the job done.

Extreme magical thinking occurs in persons who pretend

they have reached a goal, when, in fact, they have not. This deception may be so successful that the person not only convinces others, but also convinces himself. This pretending reaches psychotic proportion when it is obvious to everyone except the pretender. For example, a man may believe that he discovered electricity, and he might become irate when others fail to recognize his greatness.

A milder degree of pretending occurs in persons who claim they have training or skills that they don't have. The so-called *impostor syndrome* refers to persons pretending to be skilled professionals, such as physicians or attorneys. They may or may not have bogus degrees from diploma mills. Most of them know that they are living a lie. But others convince themselves of their own lies and truly believe they have the claimed skills.

Years ago, a friend had often described to me in vague but exciting terms his adventures as a pilot. One day he accepted my invitation to go flying with me (at the time I was a flight instructor). Imagine my consternation when I observed that he knew nothing about piloting a plane. He could not start the engine or steer the plane on the ground. In spite of the compelling evidence that he did not have a clue about piloting a plane, this man continued to maintain that he was a seasoned pilot, explaining that he was a "bit rusty."

Let's face it, there are no shortcuts to achieving difficult goals. Our mature parts must be involved to develop timelines and realistic steps to achieve them. The magical thinking of childhood will not accomplish the task.

Time Lines

To reach goals, you must translate them into **tangible actions occurring at specific times**. Without actions, goals remain fantasies. Without timelines, the actions may never occur.

Develop timelines by identifying subgoals, or specific steps to achieve your goal. Translate these steps into actions. Then estimate how long each action will take. You can modify the estimate, based on experience. Once you have estimated the time required for each step, you will have a rough idea of when you can expect to achieve your goal. Use your calendar to see how the plan for reaching the goal fits with other scheduled activities. Then enter each step in your goal action plan on your calendar. This integrates your goal and the steps needed for its achievement into the reality of scheduled daily activities.

Your goal begins to become reality when you assign specific times on your weekly schedule to action steps that are parts of your goal plan. If you are not using a weekly schedule, begin doing so, since it is key to taking charge of your life. List the hours you plan to be awake for each day of the week. Then assign a specific activity to each time slot (usually an hourly schedule works well). Develop the schedule for the following week each weekend, so that this process becomes part of your routine. You might schedule some activities weeks, or even months, ahead of time. And you might factor others into your schedule a day or two ahead of time. Be flexible in adapting to unexpected priorities.

Using this approach, goal-related activities (including leisure time) will be scheduled at specific times for each day. Throughout the day, base your actions on this schedule rather than on your feelings. Then your goals will govern how you use your time.

Here is an example of one day's schedule in my current life:

6:00 a.m.	Out of bed, 45 minutes vigorous exercise, shower, shave, etc.
7:00 a.m.	Time socializing with cats and wife.
8:00 a.m.	Work on book.

10:00 a.m.	Leave for office.
10:15 a.m.	Begin office telephone calls, paperwork, review of cases, etc.
11:00 a.m.	Interview applicants for police departments.
11:30 a.m.	Patient.
12:30 p.m.	Lunch meeting.
1:30 p.m.	Phone calls and paperwork.
2:00 p.m.	Patients until 7:00 p.m..
7:00 p.m.	Drive home, fix snack, socialize with wife and cats, take care of cats' (many) needs.
8:00 p.m.	Snack, read journals, books, and/or newspaper. Socialize with wife and cats.
10:00 p.m.	Watch news, get ready for bed, meditate, sleep.

Celebrate!

Congratulate yourself for every goal you reach, since behavior is strengthened with reinforcement. And don't limit yourself to major goals; if you do, you won't have many celebrations. Get in the habit of stroking yourself for achieving even small, unimportant goals, so that rewarding yourself becomes a strong habit. Not only will this increases your goal-directed activity, it will also improve your self-esteem.

How you celebrate will be a matter of personal preference, and may vary with the importance of the goal. For example, I give myself a small "attaboy" whenever I complete a paragraph of this book. A larger "Yes! Great!" follows completion of a chapter. I don't know yet how I will celebrate completion of the whole book, but I know that my creative parts will come up with something nice. And when the book is published, I'll really go wild!

The following outline can be a useful guide in developing goals.

GOAL SETTING FORM

My specific goal is:

Do I really *want* it?Is it *tangible*?
Is it *realistic*?Is it *challenging*?
Is it consistent with my *values*?

Benefits of achieving this goal:

To me:
To others:

My timetable for reaching this goal:

I will begin work on this goal:
I will have achieved this goal:

Obstacles to reaching this goal:

External obstacles:
Internal obstacles:

Ways that I will overcome these obstacles:

External obstacles:
Internal obstacles:

How will I know when I have achieved this goal?

How will others know when I have achieved this goal?

Resources I will use to reach this goal:

Personal resources (e.g., skills, experiences):
External resources (e.g., people, groups, books):

I am making the following decision(s) to accomplish this goal:

(e.g., I *will* exercise three times a week)

Goals and Beliefs

The power of beliefs was discussed in Chapter 3. If we cling to irrational beliefs about how things should be and/or how things are, they may control important parts of our life. Such beliefs can, for example, sabotage goals.

Sabotaging Goals:

Here is an example of how someone keeps sabotaging an important goal by repeating actions, based on irrational beliefs, which do not work. Whenever Dave's girlfriend tells him that she is going out with friends, he asks her such questions as "Who are these friends?" "Any single men or women?" "When will you be back?" "What will you be doing?" and so forth. Usually, his girlfriend gets irritated and angry. And Dave becomes increasingly demanding in getting answers. He also lets her know, often by pouting or acting angry, that he doesn't want her going out with friends without him. This pattern recurs repeatedly, and it usually ends with the girlfriend leaving an angry Dave.

Dave's actions are sabotaging his goal of having a secure, close relationship with a woman. On the contrary, the pattern usually drives women away. Dave's efforts to keep a woman with him and away from other men stem from his irrational beliefs, which include beliefs about the Perceived World that: "People I love will leave me" and "I am basically unlovable (and that's why others leave me when they really know me)." He also holds a Fantasy World belief that "When someone really loves you, they should want to spend all the time they can with you." Based on these crazy beliefs, Dave decided long ago that "I must control the one I love and keep her from contact with other men." Obviously, this decision is not working. First, it is irrational, since it is impossible to control another adult. And second, it leads to negative consequences, since it drives women away rather than bringing them closer.

When you keep sabotaging an important goal, realize that you are operating from one or more irrational beliefs. Welcome this opportunity to revisit your beliefs so that you can, if you choose, replace irrational beliefs with rational ones.

Beliefs and Decisions

Rather than basing decisions on goals, we often decide on the basis of feelings generated by irrational beliefs. These decisions typically lead to negative consequences. So it can be useful to discover these goal-defeating decisions. Once you have identified a decision that is not working for you, resist the temptation to criticize yourself for having made a poor decision. Remember that self-criticism is an expression of the Osiris Factor that contributes to low self-esteem and to depression. Instead, congratulate yourself on having uncovered a decision that is no longer working. Recognize that when you made the decision (often when you were a child), it probably made sense and was the best decision you could make at the time.

Write down the decision that is no longer working for you. In Dave's example above, he might write down:

- "I must control the one I love."

After listing the decision that is not working, replace it with a new decision. Develop a decision that is more rational, more likely to work for you, and more likely to lead to appropriate feelings. You might replace the irrational decision listed above with the following decision:

"I might do what I can to *influence* others, realizing that it's impossible to control them, and that trying to do so is neither desirable nor realistic."

Once you've made a re-decision, it's going to take time and practice to translate it into new behavior. To do so, you'll have to replace old habits with new ones. Initially, this is difficult and feels unnatural and forced. That's all right. Learn to tolerate the discomfort; the result will be well worth the effort. And remember to congratulate yourself for each small gain you make.

Let's apply these principles to the previous example of Dave, who is trying to control his partner. Next time he fears losing her, he might bite his tongue and resist the urge to question her. He will probably still feel anxiety, but if he doesn't say anything, he might congratulate himself for making progress. Then, he could remind himself that trying to control her is driving her away. He might also recall that he is a lovable person, so there is no rational reason to believe that she will leave him. But in spite of these wise words to himself, Dave will probably continue to feel anxiety for some time about this situation.

It usually takes longer for feelings to change than for behavior and thoughts to change. **So reaching goals often requires acting from goals and rational new beliefs and decisions rather than from feelings or habits**. This requires effort and practice, and in the early stages may seem forced and "unnatural."

Next time Dave's mate tells him that she is going out with friends, he might tell himself "The evidence is strong that she cares for me" and "I'm a decent, lovable person." At first, he won't "really" believe this. But with repetition, he gradually will accept this new way of interpreting the situation.

SIX

REPROGRAMMING THE OSIRIS FACTOR

June shakes her head and presses both fists against her eyes, as if to stem the flow of tears coursing down her cheeks. "I didn't mean to do anything wrong," she wails to her good friend, Nancy, who nods sympathetically. "I don't know what's wrong with me. No matter how hard I try, it's never good enough!" She gasps between sobs. "My husband's never satisfied, and I just can't please him. I know I should try harder, but I get so tired!"

"You're just plain lazy." Victoria points an accusing finger at her 10-year-old son, who slouches on the couch, peering avidly at the TV. "I'm not going to put up with your sloppiness anymore! I expect some help around here, and I'm not going to be your servant, let me tell you... "

June and Victoria are both acting from the Osiris Factor. June judges herself as wrong; Victoria judges her son as wrong. The Osiris Factor operates whenever we decide that someone (our self or another person) is not acting in accordance with our Fantasy World. Having judged someone *wrong*, we then conclude that the person (our self and/or another) *should* change.

As previously discussed, we are all programmed from an early age to respond to many of our experiences as if we were God. We learn to constantly judge whether we or others are right or wrong, good or bad, healthy or unhealthy, functional or dysfunctional, and so forth. Once we have adopted this judgmental approach to life, it becomes increasingly automatic, like any other frequently used habit.

Our Fantasy World determines the intensity of our "shoulding" and what triggers it. For example, if we have irrational beliefs about pleasing others, when we believe that we are not pleasing others, we will "should" on ourselves and generate guilt. If we base our self-esteem on being pleasers, and conclude that we are failing in this role, we will develop shame and our self-esteem will decline. Both guilt and shame will foster depression.

On the other hand, if we have irrational beliefs about how others should treat us, we will often "should" on them. For example, if in our Fantasy World people treat us fairly, when we conclude that someone is treating us unfairly, we will "should" on them and generate anger.

The **major characteristics of the Osiris Factor** include the following:

- We **judge** others and/or ourselves.
- We assign **blame** and **fault**.
- We decide who is **right** and who is **wrong**.
- In relationships, we tend to be **critical, contemptuous, defensive**, and/or **withdrawn**.
- We think in terms of polarities, such as **either/or, all/nothing,** and so forth.
- We experience life as a series of **trials** and **prosecutions**.
- We generate intense **anger, guilt, shame,** and/or **depression**.
- We use words like **should, need to, ought to, must, right/wrong, good/bad, and why?** (*Why* questions are usually disguised *shoulds* rather than genuine requests for information. So "Why didn't you call me?" means "You should have called me," and "Why do you keep spending so much?" means "You shouldn't spend so much.")

Giving Up Godhood

If you want to reduce anger, shame, guilt, and/or depression, you must give up godhood. Indeed, some biblical scholars have interpreted the passage in Genesis dealing with Adam and Eve eating of the fruit of the tree of good and evil ("original sin" or "the Fall") as symbolic of man's desire to become like God and to usurp God's role as judge (Borg, 2001). But relinquishing this approach to life is a lot easier said than done. For most of us, Osiris-type thinking has become a firmly established habit, which we use hundreds of times per day. Such learned habits become *automatic*, occur *without awareness*, and operate *very quickly*.

To reduce such habits, you must become aware of them. Because they occur so quickly, during the early stages of change, most people will only catch the habit after it has begun. Suppose that you have developed the habit of tugging one of your ears, and that you have been doing this for years, hundreds of times a day. Now you decide to reduce this habit. You will find that, at first, you will occasionally catch yourself tugging the ear. You might even be surprised that you are tugging, not recalling deciding to do so. That's what I mean by automatic. While you might not be able to prevent the habit, you can eliminate it when you become aware of it.

This principle applies to reducing the Osiris Factor. When you first decide to reduce this habit, you will often find yourself under its spell before you realize it. At that point, immediately relinquish Osiris's throne ("I am not God. It's not my role to judge.") As you do so, the negative feelings that you have been generating will gradually decline.

With practice, the time you spend under the sway of the Osiris Factor will decrease, resulting in shorter and less intense periods of anger, guilt, shame, and/or depression. Eventually, you will avoid assuming the role of Osiris in the first place. This happy change will occur gradually and imperfectly. You will avoid godhood in some situations and not in others.

Detecting the Osiris Factor will probably be a challenge. One of the best signs that you have come under its influence is the emergence of the negative feelings that it generates. Therefore, pay attention to anger, guilt, shame, and depression. When you detect one or more of these feelings, suspect that you are triggering the Osiris Factor.

Another good indication of the Osiris Factor is the use of the words, listed above (under "Characteristics of the Osiris Factor"), which are characteristic of Osiris thinking. Pay attention to your use of these words, both in talking with people and in your internal self-talk.

But once you have identified the Osiris Factor, what do you do then? That will depend on what you find works best for you. I find that an effective approach is to immediately tell myself, *"There's nothing wrong with that!"* Other self-statements can follow, depending on the situation.

This strategy may reveal another difficulty in overcoming the Osiris Factor. As you tell yourself "There's nothing wrong with that," you may think: "But there *is* something wrong with it!" You may then justify your judgment. This places you squarely back in the role of a god who knows how things are and how they should be. As you muster evidence to justify your judgment, you increase the negative feelings of anger, shame, guilt, and/or depression.

When you tell yourself that someone (including yourself) "really" is wrong, you have identified one or more of your Fantasy World beliefs. You are clinging to an irrational belief, and you are refusing to accept reality. Therefore, exploring how you maintain the Osiris Factor can reveal Fantasy World beliefs. A previous chapter (Chapter 3) has dealt in greater detail with beliefs, and how you can change irrational Fantasy World and Perceived World beliefs into more realistic and useful beliefs. Remember that it takes time and effort to change beliefs, so be patient with yourself.

But deleting the Osiris Factor from your habitual approach to life is not enough. You need to replace this destructive habit with another habit that will work better for you (and the people with whom you relate).

Hello, Humility

We can replace the Osiris Factor with what I call the **Humility Factor**. When we surrender our fantasies of being God and accept that our version of how things should be and how they are is no better than anyone else's, we stop judging, blaming, and criticizing the world for being what it is. Rather than going through life as a judge, we assume the posture of a scientist. As a scientist, we **observe** with interest what happens in our life. We **accept** whatever happens, whether we like it or not. Instead of judging whether something is right or wrong, we decide whether what we are doing is **working or not working** in helping us to reach our goals.

Judgments of whether something or someone is right or wrong are usually based on comparing our Perceived World with our Fantasy World. Deciding whether something is working or not working is based on observing whether it is helping us to achieve our **goals**. We do not judge others or ourselves. But we may decide that some of our behavior or the behavior of others is not to our liking (which does not make it wrong).

The **major characteristics of the Humility Factor** can be summarized as follows:

- We **observe** others and ourselves with interest.
- We **accept** others and ourselves as reality. We tell ourselves "That's the way it is, although I might not always like it."
- We notice whether our actions **work or do not work**, depending on whether they help us to reach our **goals**.
- We listen to others and ourselves with empathy and respect.
- We think in terms of **degrees and shades of gray**, instead of in terms of all or nothing.
- We think in terms of **both/and** instead of either/or.
- We view life as a series of **experiments** (how well do various approaches work?) and **learning opportunities**, instead of a series of court trials.
- We generate a wealth of useful **knowledge** based on our experience, leading to increasing **wisdom**.
- Humility Factor words include: I **prefer**, I **wish**, I **choose**, I **decide**, I **like/don't like**, I **will/won't**, and so forth. Notice that these words empower us, whereas Osiris Factor words foster passivity and powerlessness (we are ruled by our grandiosity and our version of Fantasy World).

Although the Osiris Factor generates negative feelings, it does not necessarily lead to action. When it does, the action is often impulsive and counterproductive. The Humility Factor, on the other hand, leads to action that is goal-directed. Remember that you do not need to be angry to influence people. And you do not need to feel guilt or shame to make personal changes.

The following table presents a comparison of the Osiris Factor and the Humility Factor approaches to life:

Comparing Osiris and Humility Factors

OSIRIS FACTOR	HUMILITY FACTOR
Judging	Observing
Blaming	Accepting
Right/wrong	Works/doesn't work
Criticism, Contempt	Empathy/respect
Defensiveness	Self-disclosure
Either/or	Both/and
All/nothing	Degrees/percentages
Trials	Experiments/learning
Anger and/or depression	Wisdom/action
Powerless words	Powerful words

SEVEN

GOOD-BYE TO ANGER

Although popular with many people, anger can have devastating consequences, such as marital failure, homicide, child abuse, hate crimes, terrorism, and genocide. And people often focus their anger on those they love most, as attested to by the almost million cases of domestic violence reported yearly.

Yet, many people cherish anger, and some even pride themselves on having a bad temper or a "short fuse." Some people believe their temper is innate and can't be changed. They want others, especially loved ones, to accept their temper. And they expect others to comply with their wishes, so as not to "make" them mad.

Such bad-tempered people often say things like, "She knows not to push my buttons, but she keeps doing it, so of course I get mad!" "If only he wouldn't bother me when I'm in one of those moods, I wouldn't keep going off on him." "She knows what makes me mad, but she keeps doing it anyway. Why does she do that?!" Notice that, in each of these statements, the implication is that someone else is responsible for the anger, and that this person <u>should change</u>. Here is the Osiris Factor in full bloom.

Since people sometimes get their way with anger, it is no wonder that they cherish this skill and that they keep using it. This occasional reinforcement probably explains why it is so difficult to weaken and replace the anger habit. Research has shown that habits that are reinforced occasionally and unpredictably are generally more resistant to change than habits that are reinforced consistently (Skinner, 1938).

The Fruits of Anger

If getting angry gets you what you want, why stop? The problem is that, while anger may work in the short term, its longterm consequences may be the opposite of what you want. That is, anger often wins battles while losing wars.

The usual response to anger is to withdraw or to get angry in return. When you get angry with someone, he or she will usually retaliate with anger or will comply with your demands. But in either case, the person will gradually withdraw from you, if not physically, then emotionally.

Withdrawal may be insidious, perhaps occurring over a period of years. For example, Don and Carol have been married 20 years, and Don thought the marriage was working well until he discovered, to his amazement, that Carol was having an affair. He felt wronged and betrayed. As counseling with me proceeded, Carol revealed that she had been afraid of her husband's anger for years. Although she sometimes complied ("to keep the peace"), and she sometimes expressed anger, she gradually withdrew from Don. Her love for him was slowly replaced with fear and resentment. Eventually, she stopped loving him and went through the motions of the marriage. The affair was the culmination of Carol's emotional withdrawal from Don.

Now Don understands his mistakes, wishes to make amends, and wants to resume the marriage. He no longer gets angry with Carol and treats her the way she had always asked him to treat her. But it is too late. She has disengaged from him emotionally and no longer feels about him "that special way." She does not trust his dramatic change. And she wonders if it is genuine, or if the old patterns will reappear once Don again feels secure in the relationship. She also asks why, if he can now change his temper with relative ease, he didn't do it years ago. She's been pleading with him to stop being angry for a long time. She concludes that he is changing now only because he fears losing her. His anger has lost him his wife; he won many battles, but he lost the war.

Thinking Yourself Out of Anger

The first step in reducing anger is to genuinely choose to do so. Unless you **strongly commit yourself to abandoning anger**, you will continue to use it automatically. Realizing that anger is undermining your important relationships and making you feel miserable will help you to firmly decide to stop angering yourself.

The second step in overcoming anger is to understand that **you make yourself angry**. As long as you blame others for your anger and believe that you have no choice in reacting to what others say or do, you are powerless to change it. Recognizing that it is your godlike judgment of others (the Osiris Factor) that generates anger enables you to start taking charge of it. You can learn to change your interpretation of situations.

The basic program for anger, as already outlined, consists of deciding that **someone or something is "wrong" and "should" be different**. It is that simple and uninteresting. It boils down to deciding that the world as you perceive it must change to conform to your fantasy of how it should be (your Fantasy World), or deciding that your interpretation of how things are (your Perceived World) is right while someone else's interpretation is wrong. In other words, it is the application of the Osiris Factor to other people.

Anger is based on grandiosity—the erroneous belief that you have powers and wisdom far greater than other mortals. It is based on the misconception that you know how things are and how they should be, and that you have the right to insist that others agree and comply with your views.

The third step to stop angering yourself is to surrender the belief that your fantasy of how the world should be is right. Instead, think of it as your *preference*. It is how you would like things to be, not how they should be. Then, **shift to the Humility Factor** and recognize that other people have as much right to their fantasies about the world as you do. They have as much right to their beliefs as you have to yours.

You might argue that when you feel strongly about a belief, you would prefer that others who are important to you share this belief. Living with them would be easier and more pleasant. This is probably accurate, but it does not justify your insisting that they should, therefore, agree with you.

Suppose, for example, that you believe that marriage partners should be honest with each other. If your partner shares this belief, you will probably be pleased when she is honest with you. But suppose that you find her lying to you. Your old pattern would have been to conclude that she is wrong and that she should change. You would have made yourself angry, alienating yourself from her. Angry and/or afraid of you, she might have become even less honest with you.

From the Humility Factor, you would accept what you interpret as your partner's lying as neither right nor wrong. Instead, you would consider it behavior that you would prefer were different. Instead of making yourself angry about it, you would ask yourself what *action* you might take that could influence your partner to behave more consistently with your preference, without alienating her and undermining your goal of a rewarding relationship.

I am not suggesting that you abandon all hope of influencing events or people. Most of us can occasionally influence some people. Feeling bad, however, is not an effective way of doing this. As previously noted, anger influences others to withdraw from us. It also reduces our ability to think clearly. Clear thinking helps us to influence others, while anger typically reduces our influence with people.

Actions and Feelings

The solution to anger is to not generate it, to resist the temptation to judge someone as wrong and "should" on the culprit. However, since countless repetitions have made the Osiris Factor automatic and virtually instantaneous, it is unrealistic to expect to change such a well-established habit overnight. Therefore, early in your campaign of changing this habit, learn how to **act calm while feeling angry**. Thus, you can control your behavior while still learning to change your thinking.

Most people already know how to do this. They may do it daily. If they get angry with their boss, for example, they may act calm. But if they get angry with someone they love (such as their mate or children), they may act angry. They are choosing to act angry in one case and to act calm in another.

If you already know how to act calm while feeling angry, start practicing doing this with the persons who are most important to you. Although you may have this skill, you may not know how you do it. In that case, when you begin to anger yourself at someone who is important to you, **imagine that person is your boss**, or someone else with whom you act calm when feeling angry.

Also try the following two techniques, which can help you to act calm while feeling angry. With Pausing Breath, as soon as you begin to feel angry, take a deep diaphragmatic breath, count slowly to three, and exhale slowly. As you exhale, tell yourself "relax and think," and let your muscles get as limp as possible. With practice, this can become an automatic response to your initial awareness of anger. It interrupts the physical and mental expressions of anger, and it gives you time to replace the Osiris Factor with the Humility Factor. Even if you have not yet mastered this habit substitution, you can remind yourself of your goal of acting calm, although you may continue to feel angry.

Another simple technique to avoid acting angry is to call a **Time Out** when you *begin* to feel angry. For this to work, you and your partner must have agreed that as soon as either one of you begins to feel angry, that person calls "Time Out," and the other partner accepts it without argument. Both partners drop the topic under discussion, and they introduce no other controversial issue. The person who has called the Time Out is responsible for calling "time in" when he feels calm again, but no sooner than 20 minutes. It takes at least this long for our bodies to calm down again. His partner is then free to agree or to disagree to resume the discussion at that point.

For Time Out to work, it must be used as soon as you begin to feel angry. It is likewise essential that both partners honor the procedure. Sometimes one partner feels compelled to resolve the issue on the spot and refuses to stop the discussion. Unfortunately, this well-meant approach seldom works. As anger mounts, reason declines, reducing the likelihood of resolving the conflict.

What you do mentally during the Time Out will determine its success. If you elaborate on the theme that your partner is wrong and should change, you will continue to anger yourself. You may, indeed, increase anger during the Time Out. For it to work, you must replace the anger program with rational thinking. That is, you must accept your partner without judgment and remind yourself of your **goal** (such as closeness to your partner). Remember, too, that anger is not likely to cause the change you want; instead, it will probably make things worse. If the change you want is unrealistic, accept things as they are without anger.

Fantasy World and Anger

Anger occurs when we find a discrepancy between our Perceived World and our Fantasy World, and we start "shoulding" on the Perceived World. We can replace the shoulding program with the more useful and realistic program of accepting the world as it is. We can facilitate this difficult change by **modifying our Fantasy World so that it is more realistic.**

In chapter 3, I presented a partial list of popular Irrational Beliefs. Many of them predispose us to anger by leading to unrealistic expectations of how other people should act (for example, fairly, honestly, reasonably, respectfully, charmingly, responsibly, and so forth).

You can identify the irrational beliefs underlying your anger by asking yourself how you decide that someone or something is wrong. The answer will reveal one or more irrational beliefs. Whenever these beliefs are violated, you are likely to anger yourself. Changing these beliefs to more rational beliefs, as previously discussed, will reduce the opportunities for you to anger yourself.

Here is an example of how this approach might be applied:

- You discover yourself getting angry when someone you love interrupts you.

-**Anger program**: He's wrong for interrupting me.

-**Why is he wrong?**

- He's wrong because interrupting me is disrespectful, and he should respect me, and he should want to know what I'm thinking.

-**Irrational beliefs**:

- People should respect me.
- People who love me should want to know what I am thinking.

-**Rational beliefs**:

- I like it when people respect me, and I accept the fact that sometimes people don't.
- People who love me will sometimes be interested in what I'm thinking.

Anger Movies

As discussed in Chapter 4, we spend time in trances, focusing on internal fantasies and/or memories, instead of attending to external events. When in a trance, our feelings are usually appropriate to the inner movies which we are viewing.

To maintain or intensify anger, we can play movies in which we interpret other people's actions as wrong. The more convinced we are of the wrongness of the actions, the angrier we will be. People who are skilled at anger usually have a rich movie collection of situations in which they were wronged, often by important people in their lives. These movies are not limited to recent events. We can anger ourselves about memories of our distant past as easily as about events that occurred yesterday. And we are likely to keep editing the movies (unconsciously) to reinforce our belief that we were wronged.

Angry clients often tell me that they "carry a lot of anger from the past." They believe that this reservoir of anger, accumulated over years, keeps seeking discharge. They sometimes think that, if they discover the "real source" of the anger, they will no longer be angry. I believe, instead, that we **recreate** anger each time we review a memory and repeat the shoulding process.

Venting anger about past events does not eliminate it. In fact, it often increases anger. It only decreases when, for whatever reason, we stop replaying the old movies and stop "shoulding" on their featured actors. The solution to anger stemming from past events is not venting the anger. You stop being angry about a past event when you stop telling yourself how wrong it was and how it should have been different. That is, when you replace the Osiris Factor with the Humility Factor.

We can increase anger toward someone with movies that trigger additional anger, such as movies of prior events in which the person "was wrong." Or we can use movies in which someone else was wrong. Usually, when using movies of someone other than the person with whom we are currently angry, we justify the movie selection by finding a connection between the current perpetrator's behavior and the past situation.

For example, you might anger yourself toward your husband because he forgot to pick up the cleaning. You might tell yourself, "He's wrong for forgetting that. It's because he's so selfish (and it's wrong to be selfish). He's just like my third husband!" And you can now continue to increase your anger with movies of the third husband's many wrong-doings.

If you want to reduce anger, monitor your internal movies. Avoid playing those which you interpret as someone's wrong-doing. Furthermore, identify "oldies and goodies" that you replay frequently, so that you can dispose of them. A mental health professional can help you to dispose of old movies that keep resurfacing. Or you might handle these movies on your own. In either case, your goal is to trash the movies and to stop angering yourself with them.

You can also use trances to reduce anger. Replay movies of times that you responded calmly to anger triggers. By reviewing these scenes repeatedly, you can strengthen the habit of acting calm although feeling angry.

Even more useful is making movies of new ways of dealing with situations that, in the past, triggered your anger. You can imagine someone pressing one of your most potent anger triggers. Then, instead of shifting into the familiar anger program, tell yourself something like, "There's nothing wrong with that. It's just different from the way I would like it to be, and it's reality." Then, imagine yourself taking a Pausing Breath and calmly dealing with the situation. The more you rehearse this scene, the stronger your new response will become. And the more likely you will be to cope with similar future situations without anger. You will thereby weaken the Osiris Factor and strengthen the Humility Factor.

Comparing the Osiris and Humility Factors

The following example illustrates how the Osiris Factor escalates anger while the Humility Factor reduces or prevents it. Words or statements that indicate the operation of either of these factors are in bold print. Underlying beliefs and/or thoughts are in italics. These beliefs and/or thoughts are not always immediately available to awareness, since they have become automatic with frequent repetition.

Imagine yourself frustrated and hurt because you have been feeling neglected by your partner. You decide to discuss this issue with him/her. Compare the following two scenarios that may result from the Osiris or the Humility Factor.

Osiris Factor	**Humility Factor**
You: We **need** to talk. (*I know what's needed for both of us*).	You: **I'd like** to talk to you about something that's important to me (It may not be important to my partner).
Partner: Not now. Can't you see I'm watching this TV program?	Partner: Not now. Can't you see I'm watching this TV program?
You: **Why** is that TV program more important to you than our relationship? (It *shouldn't* be! *He/she's being selfish again, and he shouldn't be!)*	You: Of course. Please let me know when it might be a good time for us to talk. (My partner has the right to prioritize how he/she wants to use his/her time, and that may have nothing to do with his/her feelings toward me.)
Partner: **There you go again!** Making a big thing out of everything! We can talk when the program's over. (Both of you are already angry.)	Partner: I'll be glad to talk with you when the program's over (Neither of you is angry).
You: (Program has ended) You've been neglecting me and being selfish again, and I want to know **why**. (*I know he/she's being selfish, and he/she shouldn't be selfish. And my partner should be honest with me and answer my questions directly.)*	You: (Program has ended) I'm sure that you really care for me, and lately I've been feeling neglected and I'm feeling hurt. (I would like my partner to be more attentive and spend more time with me.)

Partner: I don't know what you're talking about. I'm constantly doing things for you, but it's never enough! **All you do is complain and criticize.**	Partner: I didn't realize that you felt that way. I care for you and don't want you to feel hurt. **What can I do to make things better for you?**
You: There you go again! You **never** understand what I'm feeling, you're so into yourself! *(He/she has always been like this, and it's wrong, and he/she should change and make me feel good instead of bad).*	You: **I would like** you to spend more time with me and tell me about what is going on with you. (That would be really nice, and my partner may or may not agree to cater to my preferences, and that's all right either way.)

Notice how negatively this scenario develops when you operate from the Osiris Factor and insist that your Fantasy World should prevail (your partner should want to talk with you when you choose and should want to spend time with you and cater to your feelings) and that your Perceived World is the right interpretation of things (your partner is selfish and never understands your feelings). Although you won't get what you want from your partner every time that you request a change using the Humility Factor, your chances will be better. More importantly, with the Osiris Factor you and your partner generate anger; with the Humility Factor, you won't generate anger, and your partner is less likely to do so. You are likely to foster a closer relationship with your partner with the Humility Factor, and you are likely to distance yourself from your partner with the Osiris Factor.

What's Wrong with Anger?

This chapter might appear to be an indictment of anger.

This is not my intent. Anger is a natural emotion that can be useful as well as destructive. It is the natural, automatic reaction to sudden, unexpected pain. For example, if I bump my head against an open cupboard door, the immediate reaction is likely to be anger. It is typically immediate and brief, unless I activate the Osiris Factor and insist that I shouldn't have hit my head, that the door shouldn't have been left open, and so forth.

Like all emotions, anger can provide useful information. Typically, it tells us that we want something to change. It can be useful to explore what that might be. Having discovered what we want to change, we can assess whether the change is realistic, and whether the required time and effort will be worth the potential benefit. Often, continuing to generate anger will reduce, rather than increase, the likelihood of achieving the change we desire.

Since anger is usually a reaction to pain and/or fear, dealing with those emotions might be useful. People you care for are more likely to accept your pain or fear than your anger. While anger drives others away, genuine pain or fear doesn't usually have this effect. By dealing with your pain or fear, you will probably resolve the issue that is triggering your anger.

Suppose, for example, that your mate tells you that he plans to go fishing with some buddies on a day you had hoped to spend with him. If you anger yourself ("He is wrong for not wanting to spend time with me, and he **should** want to spend that time with me!") and criticize him for being selfish, thoughtless, and so forth, he will probably react angrily and defensively. The result will be further alienation. On the other hand, if you say something like, "I can understand your wanting to go out with your buddies. And I feel a little sad and disappointed, because I had hoped to spend the day with you," your mate is more likely to respond positively. He might even change his fishing plans or make plans with you for another day.

Once you realize that you want something to change, ask yourself why you want it to be different. Resist the temptation to answer, "Because it's wrong!" Remember, that's how you make yourself angry. And your idea of what is wrong and another person's idea of what is wrong are matters of personal opinion or preference. Don't try to justify your preference for a change by clinging to the right/wrong way of thinking. Instead, explore fears or hurts that you might be trying to avoid or reduce by the desired change. As noted above, telling another of your fears or hurts and requesting a change is more likely to produce the desired change than is anger. Furthermore, keep in mind that, although anger may bring you the immediate change you want, it eventually pushes others away.

In some situations, however, anger can work well. For example, anger usually works when our goal is to distance another person from us, either temporarily or permanently. It can also work well when our goal is to intimidate another person with whom we don't plan to maintain a continuing relationship. Finally, anger is useful when we need maximum physical strength without also needing a high level of skill or coordination. Anger increases sheer strength, but reduces fine coordination and the ability to think clearly.

Shared anger can sometimes lead to constructive group action. The action, and not the anger, may achieve impressive goals. It is not necessary to be angry to act. Generally, anger reduces the effectiveness of actions, and sometimes completely undermines them.

EIGHT

OVERCOMING DEPRESSION

Millions of people are depressed at some time in their life. It is one of the most common results of the Osiris Factor. Programming for depression begins early in life and is constantly strengthened by society. Reinforcement also comes from those around us and from our own beliefs and habits of thinking. Severity of depression varies from person to person and from time to time. Although some of us are more prone to it than others, most people occasionally inadvertently trigger some depression.

Sadness and Depression

Depression is one of three forms of sadness. Unfortunately, even some professionals refer to any sad feelings as depression. This confuses the issue and may lead to improper treatment. The three basic types of sad feelings may exist singly or in any combination.

Unhappiness

I use the term unhappiness to refer to the **normal**, appropriate response to negative events in our lives and/or lack of positive events. Our level of happiness/unhappiness is a useful gauge of how well life is going for us and how much we are enjoying it. It varies with our life experiences. Since much of what happens to us is not under our control, it is unrealistic to expect constant happiness. If you should lose a large sum of money, find that someone has burglarized your house, discover that your car needs a new engine, or notice that it is raining hard just as you are planning an exciting golf game, you will probably not react with happiness. If you did, your reaction would be—to put it kindly—a bit strange. When a client tells me that he has no hobbies, leisure time interests, or good friends, I suspect that he may be unhappy, although not necessarily depressed.

To increase happiness, you may need to **make life changes**. Increasing positive experiences and/or decreasing negative experiences will increase happiness. This requires being proactive and taking personal responsibility for increasing your happiness. As long as you wait passively for events to change your life ("when I get a promotion," "after I graduate," "when the right one comes along," and so forth), you will probably stay stuck in your current rut.

Likewise, expecting others to change ("when my wife stops nagging," "when my husband spends more quality time with me," "when my boss supports me," and so forth) gives them control of your life and responsibility for your happiness, which is bad news! Since you can't control others, basing your happiness on their actions makes you vulnerable and leads to feeling powerless and helpless, which contributes to depression.

Increase happiness in your life by adding positive experiences to each day's schedule. These experiences need not be major events. Identify simple, realistic things you can do that you enjoy. For example, plan to spend a few minutes listening to your favorite music, schedule lunch with a friend, play with your cat, or enjoy a leisurely walk.

You can also increase happiness by reducing negative events in your life. Again, this requires action. It may require **courage** as well, since making life changes is usually scary.

Often, people remain stuck in negative situations, because they fear change. You must tolerate anxiety to take charge of your life, since change is usually scary and uncomfortable.

Suppose that your job contributes to your unhappiness. There may be valid reasons for keeping it, such as your inability to find another suitable job, great benefits, excellent opportunities for advancement, and so forth. On the other hand, being *afraid* to change jobs is not a valid reason for staying stuck in a job you despise. Fear is unavoidable with change.

Besides making life changes, you can reduce unhappiness by **focusing on positive elements in your life**, instead of dwelling on negative elements. Since we can focus on only a fraction of our experience, we can *choose* to pay attention to the positives or to the negatives. The more we emphasize the negatives, the unhappier we become. Furthermore, we can interpret situations in different ways. The tendency to judge and evaluate people and situations (the Osiris Factor) generates negative feelings. On the other hand, approaching life as an observer who is interested in learning from every experience does not generate negative feelings.

Suppose that your boss often criticizes you. You might constantly tell yourself that he is wrong for being critical, and that he shouldn't treat you this way. Or you might, instead, tell yourself that your boss is the way he is. Then experiment with different ways of coping with his criticisms, without upsetting yourself by telling yourself how wrong and awful the situation is for you. This second approach will not only feel better, but it is also more likely to have positive results.

Grief

Grief is the normal reaction to loss. We grieve the loss of people through death, end of relationships (for example, divorce), or reduced contact (such as children leaving home).

We can also grieve the loss of animal friends, cherished possessions, important parts of our lives (such as a job or the ability to engage in a favorite sport), and personal attributes or abilities.

As we pass from one life stage to another, we grieve the lost stage. In our society that cherishes youth, aging often triggers grief in response to the loss of youth. Many people struggle desperately to deny aging, using various approaches, including painful, expensive, and dangerous surgery.

So a popular approach to loss is to **deny** it, to try to fool others and ourselves into believing that the loss has not occurred. For example, a middle-aged woman may still act and dress as if she were a high school cheerleader. A college football star at 51 may still spend much time and energy trying to be a jock. Some people continue to act and feel as if a long-deceased important person, such as a parent, is still a vital part of their lives. Denial of loss can keep the person stuck in grief. He may continue to invest excessive energy and emotion in what has been lost, which may interfere with investing in living.

Grief typically includes several intense emotions, including anxiety, sadness, anger, relief, and confusion. There may also be periods of emotional numbing. Emotions typically occur in waves, which gradually occur less frequently, with decreasing intensity, and for shorter periods of time. Therefore, grief takes time and is uncomfortable and painful. It is resolved by experiencing these negative feelings and ultimately dealing with the loss and restructuring life in a meaningful way. Restructuring often involves shifting the primary focus of attention from the past to the present and future. It does not, however, require that we forget what has been lost, or that we no longer invest it with powerful feelings.

Depression

Unlike the two forms of sadness just discussed, depression is an abnormal, potentially crippling condition. Its symptoms include feelings of pain, hopelessness, worthlessness, and despair. Typically, it feeds on itself and frequently worsens without intervention.

Depression usually involves **four types of difficulties** that reinforce each other, leading to a vicious cycle. These difficulties include the following:

Cognitive Changes: Certain thought patterns initiate and increase depression. Most of us are programmed to think in ways that predispose us to depression. But some of us have had more conditioning to think this way than others. External events that we interpret as negative usually trigger these thought patterns. This is most likely when we feel powerless and helpless to control or change the events.

The depressive thought patterns are used so often they become habits that occur automatically. We often are unaware of them. We may depress ourselves and not realize that we are doing it. Many thinking patterns have been identified with depression (Beck, 1979; Burns, 1981), but I have found that most people depress themselves by using three primary thought patterns.

When someone believes that he or she is powerless to deal with a negative situation, the stage is set for depression. The most damaging thought pattern that leads to depression is **self-blame**. It is the result of the **Osiris Factor**, the **right/wrong, judgmental attitude**. The person judges herself as wrong and starts "shoulding" on herself.

If she blames herself for actions (or lack of them), the resulting feeling is **guilt**. If she blames herself for being the way she is, the resulting feeling is **shame**. Both feelings are key contributors to depression. For example, suppose that Jerry's mother criticizes him for not spending more time with her. If he tells himself, "I'm wrong for not spending more time with Mom; I really should do so," he'll experience guilt. If he then tells himself, "I'm a selfish person, and I shouldn't be this way," he'll experience shame. People who are prone to depression tend to frequently "should" on themselves, constantly generating guilt and shame. This erodes self-esteem and increases depression.

Another thought pattern that contributes to depression is the tendency to **overgeneralize**. People who are depression-prone tend to exaggerate and to use all-inclusive ideas. They magnify negative aspects of life. And they are particularly prone to magnify negative things about themselves. For example, they may say things like "*Nothing* in my life is working out," "*No one* likes me," "I *always* screw things up," "I'll *never* be good enough," "*Every* relationship in my life sucks," and so forth. By generalizing negative aspects of experience, depressed people perceive their current life as painful (Perceived World). They live under a dark cloud, because *everything* in their life seems bleak and tragic.

The third common thinking habit found in depression is to **predict a stable future**. Depressed people often think that things will *never* change. Since life is awful and terribly painful now, it will always be that way. Once this pattern is established, it leads to *hopelessness*, which leads to a sense of futility: If things will never get better, why keep trying? The "logical" solution is to give up. This line of thinking leads to loss of motivation, and, if taken to extreme, to suicidal thoughts.

Perceptual and Memory Selectiveness: People who are prone to depression have developed the habit of focusing on negative events, so that life is usually experienced as painful. More importantly, they focus on negative aspects of themselves. On the other hand, they discount or overlook positive experiences, particularly when they would reflect positively on themselves.

For example, if a man programmed for depression is told that he has done a good job, he is likely to dismiss the comment. He'll tell himself that the person making the comment is just being nice, or is trying to manipulate him, or is just "plain ignorant." On the other hand, if this man is criticized, he will tend to magnify the criticism and to obsess about it for hours, if not for days.

Memory works the same way. Memories of negative experiences are stored and easily retrieved. But memories of positive experiences are often forgotten or stored so as to be virtually unavailable. When I have asked depressed clients to tell me pleasant memories, they have often responded that they could not recall positive events in their lives.

Behavior: Depressed people tend to withdraw and isolate themselves from others. They also usually become increasingly reluctant to initiate action, appearing lethargic, unmotivated, and passive. Not surprisingly, these patterns lead to general inactivity. As withdrawal, passivity, and inactivity continue, positive life experiences decrease. This further convinces the individual that life is painful, and that he is a worthless worm.

Biological Imbalances: Many persons have biological deviations from normal functioning, most of which are temporary. Chemical imbalances, particularly in the chemistry of the brain, have been associated with depression. However, brain chemistry is in constant flux. It varies with time of day (and night), and in response to many conditions, including nutrition, hormonal changes, exercise, fatigue, activity level, and so forth. Therefore, chemical imbalances can be temporary and influenced by many variables.

Most experts agree that these four factors—cognitive,

perceptual/memory, behavioral, and biological—are important in depression. Furthermore, since these factors reinforce each other, they lead to a vicious cycle—a downward spiral, sometimes called a deep, dark pit. When we believe that we are worthless, that life is totally negative, and that there is no hope for the future, we are going to perceive and remember things in a negative way that is consistent with these beliefs. This will reinforce our negative beliefs about self and the world. With this negative outlook about self, we are naturally going to withdraw ("Who would want to be around a worm like me?") and to become passive and inactive ("No matter what I do, it's going to turn into garbage, and I won't enjoy it."). The less we do, the fewer friends we have, the more worthless we feel. These cognitive and behavioral changes will influence our brain chemistry, which will further reduce our energy, motivation, and mood. So each element involved in depression reinforces the others.

Treatment

You can take action to overcome the three types of sad emotions. You can reduce sadness if you (1) **choose** to do so, (2) **learn how** to do so, and (3) **practice** what you have learned.

Unhappiness: Unhappiness can be reduced by **increasing positive events and decreasing negative events.** Doing more of what you like and less of what you don't like will reduce unhappiness. Keep in mind that you will need courage to make life changes, since they often involve moving into unknown territory and taking risks.

Grief: Allowing yourself to *feel* your feelings will help you get through grief and eventually to *resolve the loss*. This will require time and the willingness to be uncomfortable. As you resolve your loss, you will need to *restructure your life* in a way that will help you to re-engage with life. That may require finding ways to fill the vacuum created by the loss and/or relating in new ways to what has been lost.

Depression: Although we can't live without occasional grief and unhappiness, we can live without depression. Depression is more complicated than the normal reactions of grief and unhappiness, since it is largely the result of firmly established habits. Therefore, reducing depression involves replacing old habits with new ones. And this typically takes time, effort, and practice. Here are the basic changes in habits that can eventually eliminate—or at least greatly reduce— your tendency to depression:

▪ Replace the **Osiris Factor** with the **Humility Factor**. This fundamental shift from judging to accepting will make a tremendous difference in how you experience life. Once achieved, you will stop generating anger (someone else is wrong), guilt (I acted wrongly), and shame (I am wrong). Guilt and shame contribute greatly to depression. Also refer to the chapter on self-esteem (Chapter 10), since loss of self-esteem increases depression.

▪ Replace **overgeneralizing** with thinking **specifically**. Imagine, for example, that you fail a test. You might depress yourself by telling yourself: "I didn't study hard enough, and I am to blame for failing the test (guilt). I fail at everything that's really important (overgeneralization). I am a failure (further overgeneralization, leading to shame)."

Instead of depressing yourself with these thoughts, you might tell yourself: "I failed this one test, probably because I didn't study enough. That does not mean that I fail at everything I do, and it does not mean that I am a failure. I learned from this experience that the amount of studying I did for this test did not work. Next time I'll study more and observe if that works better."

- Instead of predicting a negative future, remind yourself that **change is inevitable**, and that feelings and moods change constantly. Feeling like total garbage today does not mean that you will feel that way tomorrow. And you can greatly influence how you will feel tomorrow by how you think and how you act.
- Rather than focusing on negatives in the present and past, learn to **focus on positives** in life, and, more importantly, in yourself. When someone compliments you, develop the habit of thanking the perceptive individual. Reinforce his positive stroke by using the opportunity to review a positive belief about yourself, such as "Yes, I am a good speaker!"

Likewise, develop the habit of **making mental movies of compliments and other positive experiences**. Replay those movies often and enjoy them. On the other hand, flush negative comments and experiences down the toilet. Making movies of garbage will provide you with ammunition with which to depress yourself.

- Instead of withdrawing, being passive, and inactive, **reach out to others, be proactive, and stay active, even though you don't feel like it**.
- Consult a physician versed in treating depression for possible prescription of **antidepressant medication**. It often helps in the hard work of changing negative habits.
- Participate in regular, vigorous **exercise** (if your health permits it), even though you may not feel like it. Eat a healthy diet, sleep adequately, and take good care of your **health**.

NINE

OUR INTERNAL COMMITTEE

Pam consults me because she has been growing increasingly frustrated in her 15-year marriage. She wants to end the marriage because she feels neglected and unloved. Furthermore, she resents her husband's chronic anger and insensitivity to her emotional needs. However, when I ask her why she stays in the marriage, she explains that she loves her husband. She also fears a divorce would harm her children. Plus, she doesn't want to lose her close friendship with her in-laws. Reflecting further, she discovers that she fears being alone, does not want to risk another relationship ("which might turn out even worse!"), and believes that she might not "make it financially." Because of these conflicting thoughts and feelings, she has been deciding to stay in the marriage and to keep herself highly upset about it (primarily angry and sad).

Difficult decisions often involve internal conflict. Like Pam, we may have mixed feelings or opposite points of view about a decision. Then we may remain frozen in indecision or feel badly for whatever decision we make.

Resolving such decisions often requires awareness of how our different parts think and feel about them. It is as if we are composed of an **"internal committee"** of different parts. Each of these parts is a more or less consistent system of beliefs, attitudes, feelings, thought patterns, and behavior. There is no fixed number of committee members, and a decision may involve anywhere from a single part to many of them.

Discovering Committee Members

We can meet members of our internal committee by attending to internal conflict. The following are indications of internal conflict:

- *Indecisiveness*: When you feel "stuck" in making a decision, you may be dealing with conflict between two or more internal committee members.
- *Sabotaging Goals*: Failure to progress toward a goal is sometimes the result of self-sabotage by one or more of your committee members. When you have the ability to reach a realistic goal which you desire and you fail to make progress because of procrastination, forgetfulness, loss of motivation, and other self-generated obstacles, suspect conflict among committee members.
- *Guilt*: Guilt occurs when one or more committee members operate from the Osiris Factor and judge other members as acting, thinking, or feeling "wrong."
- *Shame*: When one or more committee members, operating from the Osiris Factor, judge other committee members as being "wrong" for being who they are, the result is shame.
- "*Accidents*": When you act in what appears to be an accidental manner that is inconsistent with your intent, it may be the result of an internal committee conflict. For example, if I intend to drive to my mother-in-law's house but "accidentally" arrive at the house of one of my good buddies, one of my committee members may have been responsible. A few minutes ago, I decided on a cup of decaffeinated coffee, but found to my surprise that I had poured a cup of caffeinated coffee (which I much prefer). I suspect the work of one of my committee members.

- *Dreams*: When you are surprised or shocked by a dream, it may reveal the operation of a committee member whose intent may be unacceptable to you when awake.
- *Inappropriate emotional reactions to another person*: Reacting strongly and inappropriately to someone may indicate that one of your irrational committee members has taken control. This may result from a similarity between the person and someone from your past about whom that committee member has unresolved issues. Or you may perceive in the person a characteristic which lurks within you but which you find unacceptable. You may then attribute to the other person (sometimes inaccurately) your own unacceptable characteristic. Committee members who reject that characteristic can then react negatively to the other person, rather than fight with another member of the committee.

Typical Committee Members

Most of us include on our internal committee members of different ages, genders, and temperaments. Some members may often take control of our actions and feelings, while others may work covertly without our awareness. Those members who are found unacceptable or "wrong" by most of the committee may be relegated to the committee's periphery, where their presence is no longer acknowledged. Yet these alienated parts of us continue to exert covert influence, often being responsible for some of the results of internal turmoil noted above. They may act as internal terrorists, terrifying and crippling us. Some eminent psychotherapists have referred to these committee members by such terms as "unconscious" or "the Shadow."

Some therapists have grouped committee members into broad categories. The categories suggested by the school of psychotherapy known as Transactional Analysis (TA, for short) can be useful in understanding internal conflicts, as well as difficulties with other people.

Here is my version of the **three basic types of committee members** posited by TA (which uses the term Ego State instead of committee member):

Child Members:

These committee members are the remnants of parts of us when we were children (primarily before the age of 8). They operate spontaneously, impulsively, and have feelings and sensations without inhibitions or controls. They cause most of our glad feelings, such as joy, excitement, and love. They are also responsible for fun and play. Other child members develop as reactions to reality or to the demands of adults or other powerful individuals (such as older siblings). These members reflect our early efforts to *adapt* to life. Some of these efforts probably worked well and helped us to function appropriately in society. Other efforts to adapt were based on the belief that there was something wrong with us, leading to the development of committee members that generate negative feelings and maladaptive or inappropriate behavior. These members are the product of the Osiris Factor.

Adult Members:

These members are the product of our ability to think logically. They anticipate consequences of our actions, and they know the difference between facts and opinions and beliefs. Adult members can think in degrees or shades of gray. On the other hand, child members think in terms of all or nothing, either/or, and black or white. Adult members usually operate from *reality* rather than from *fantasy*, as do child members. They operate much more slowly than child members. When we operate from an adult member, we must stop and think before we act.

Parent Members:

These committee members are the result of observing our parents and other parent figures during childhood. We gradually internalize our perceptions of these persons who are important to us as children. These perceptions are often distortions of the real people, reflecting the primitive thinking of our child committee members. Therefore, parent committee members operate much like child members. They function from black/white (such as right/wrong) thinking, they do not differentiate opinions and beliefs from facts, and they operate very quickly.

These members express our beliefs, values, and "shoulds." Parent members are the source of judgments, criticisms, compliments, and protective messages to ourselves and to others. They often operate from the Osiris Factor.

Conflict

Conflict among committee members leads to internal turmoil and to inconsistent feelings and behavior. Inconsistencies become evident when different members take control of our actions and feelings at different times. We might, for example, act warmly toward someone until they say something that triggers a shift in our dominant committee member, leading to a sudden wave of anger and an explosive outburst.

Consider as an example Doug, who is dedicated to start exercising (because his adult committee members think that it would make him healthier, better at sports, and more attractive to a greater percentage of women; and because parent committee members think that he would be a "better" person, be more "worthwhile," and like himself better. However, he procrastinates joining a gym and finds many excuses for not exercising (because he does not "feel" like exercising, he resents giving up watching his favorite TV programs to go to the gym, and he rebels against doing something which he feels he "should do"—all coming from child committee members).

Or take a different example, illustrating conflict between different child committee members. Bill frequently is playful and sensual with his wife (from a spontaneous, joyful child member). But whenever he feels that she neglects him, he becomes surly and angry (from a hurt and vengeful child member). His behavior puzzles and frustrates his wife. And although he may feel confused as well, Bill is likely to blame his wife for his moods, using the magical thinking of child committee members. This illustrates how child parts of us hold others responsible for our feelings and actions, operating from the Osiris Factor.

Parent committee members can also be in conflict with each other. Dave usually treats his son lovingly and respectfully (from a "positive" parent member). But whenever he interprets his son's behavior as "laziness," he becomes critical and punitive, triggering the Osiris Factor (from a "negative" parent member). Here is an example of how parent members operate from beliefs (people should not be lazy), and how they usually function, like child members, from primitive black/white thinking (laziness is bad; hard work is good). When operating from parent parts of themselves, people often confuse their beliefs with facts. So if Dave were challenged regarding his idea that laziness is bad, he might argue that this is a "truth," and that anyone who is sane would agree with him. That is, he would adopt the posture of being God, *knowing* how things should be.

Relationship conflicts can be clarified by recognizing the types of committee members involved. Imagine, for example, Joe's wife saying to him "You've done it again! You went off and didn't tell me where you were going!" She is addressing him from a parent member operating from the Osiris Factor. She is treating him like a disobedient child. Joe is likely to respond from a child member. He might apologize: "I'm so sorry, I never seem to do anything right" (a self-blaming, "I'm not good enough," depressed position). Or he might yell: "I don't have to tell you where I'm going! Get off my back!" (an angry, blaming position). On the other hand, Joe could elect to respond from an adult position. He could say, "Yes, I didn't tell you where I was going, and if that's important to you, I'll let you know in the future." Or he might respond from a parent part, stating: "Honey, please don't feel badly about it, I really want you to feel secure with me" (a positive, nurturing position). Or he could say: "Stop upsetting yourself and give me some respect!" (a critical, discounting position).

Unfortunately, most people don't know that they have a *choice* in these matters. They *automatically* respond from whatever committee member another person invites them to access. Usually, we get into most difficulty when another person approaches us from a critical, discounting parent. This invites us to respond from either a self-blaming, compliant child member, or from an angry, defensive child member. In either case, we are operating with the beliefs, attitudes, feelings, and behavior typical of a child. We are under the sway of the Osiris Factor and are likely to do and say things that we might later regret.

Decisions made from child members are usually shortsighted and the result of intense emotions. When operating from child parts, we usually act based on immediate satisfaction, without considering long-range consequences. As a result, we may sabotage longterm goals.

Let's suppose that I have a long-range goal of writing a short story. As I am tediously translating thoughts into written words, my wife invites me to join her in watching a TV program. One of my child members is activated and sabotages my writing goal by conning me with such garbage thinking as "You've done enough; you're tired; it'll do you good to relax; it'll feel good to unwind... " and so forth. If I give in to these internal "cons," my decision will be based on child wants rather than on goals.

Or consider the common example of someone who is "trying" to lose weight. Usually, people with this goal know about nutrition, but they often make moment-by-moment food decisions based on child committee members rather than based on their goal of losing weight. Good intentions are often overcome by "inner voices" saying such things as "You really want that pie!" or "You deserve that pie!" or "Just this once won't hurt you!" Such statements are "cons" from child members. If the Osiris Factor is triggered and the person starts "shoulding" on himself ("I shouldn't feel this way!"), there will be inner conflict. Usually, child members win such conflicts. The person is likely to eat the pie, and then to feel guilty about it ("I shouldn't have done that!"). The resulting guilt may then trigger further eating, to try to feel better. This pattern of feeling bad, acting from child parts for a quick feel good, feeling guilty for the action as the result of the Osiris Factor, and acting from child parts to reduce the bad feeling, is typical of addictions.

Resolving Internal Conflicts

Replacing the Osiris Factor with the Humility Factor greatly facilitates resolving both internal and interpersonal conflicts. Child and parent committee members typically operate from the Osiris Factor, while adult members are usually free of its influence. Therefore, to resolve conflicts, involve adult members of your internal committee, and let them handle key negotiations. Here is an outline of how to resolve conflict among members of the internal committee.

- *Identify all relevant committee members.* With regard to the specific decision or issue which you are working to resolve, explore all your points of view, although they may appear inconsistent or illogical. Write down each point of view to keep track of the committee members involved in the internal conflict.
- *Discover the goal or purpose of each member.* Rather than judging as per the Osiris Factor, welcome each member's point of view as interesting and worth considering. Then gently probe for each member's goal by asking yourself "How will that be useful to me?" For example, take the extreme case where one of your committee members urges you to kill someone you love. Rather than condemning that part of yourself ("I shouldn't think such things!" "What's wrong with me!" and so forth), ask that part how getting rid of your loved one might be useful to you. You might get such a response as, "Then you wouldn't have to listen to her constant nagging, and you could watch your TV programs without interruptions."
- *Validate the goal of each member.* Operating from the Humility Factor, recognize the validity of at least part of the goal or goals of each committee member. Distinguish goals from the means for reaching them. In the example above, the goals of getting less nagging and of watching TV programs without interruption may be valid goals, although the proposed means of achieving

these goals may be unacceptable. As committee members find their goals validated, they will calm down and become willing to negotiate..

- *Invite committee members to modify the means by which they try to reach their goals.* Rather than attacking a member for its point of view, encourage it to find a way of achieving at least part of its goal in ways that are acceptable to the rest of your internal committee. For example, although killing the one you love may be unacceptable to most of your internal committee, talking with her positively about your wish that she criticize you less and not interrupt some of your favorite TV programs may be an acceptable way to address the goals of the committee member which favored a homicidal option.
- *Encourage the creative members of your committee to offer compromises that will meet the goals of all interested members, at least to some degree.* Not all goals can always be met. However, most goals can be met to some degree. For example, in the case of the person who wants to lose weight, the part which wants to feel good immediately by having fattening food may be placated by participating in the selection of "healthy" food which it does enjoy. It might be further mollified by being assured that enough time will be taken to eat slowly and in a relaxed atmosphere, so that it can fully enjoy the experience.
- *Encourage Shadow members of the committee to come forth.* As you validate the goals of your committee members, those that have been ostracized and relegated to the Shadow part of the self will gradually emerge into awareness. When you become aware of them, embrace them and welcome them to the

committee meeting. Encourage them to express themselves, greeting them from the Humility Factor rather than from the Osiris Factor. Assume, for example, that as I consider whether to invite a friend for dinner I become aware of an unfamiliar sense of anxiety. When I tune in to this sense and let it expand into my awareness, I become aware of a part of me that fears that I might take advantage of my friend and use him for financial gain. Rather than reacting from the Osiris Factor ("That's awful! I'm not that kind of person, and I shouldn't be thinking this way!"), I react from the Humility Factor ("That's interesting. Let's hear more about this concern"). I may then learn about a part of me that very much wants to be wealthy (a goal that is acceptable to most of my committee) but that has felt ostracized by the dominant "altruistic" committee members. Although increasing wealth by conning or manipulating friends may not be acceptable to most of my internal committee, doing so by working cooperatively with friends may be an acceptable way of meeting the goal of the member who has been lurking in the Shadow part of the committee room.

By replacing the Osiris Factor with the Humility Factor, interpersonal conflicts can be resolved in much the same way as internal conflicts. Use the steps outlined above, replacing internal committee members with real people.

TEN

THE OSIRIS FACTOR AND THE SELF

In a recent international poll of 30,000 respondents in 30 countries, self-esteem ranked among the top five personal values listed (Johnson, 2001). Self-esteem also emerged as one of the five virtually universal roots of happiness in a recent survey of college students (O'Connor, 2001).

Self-esteem is the result of the Osiris Factor applied to the self. Most humans are programmed to judge themselves. They are constantly asking themselves "Am I good or bad?" "Am I doing the right thing?" "Am I good enough?" "How do I compare with others?" and so forth. The resulting **self-evaluation determines a person's self-esteem.**

Self-esteem varies from time to time and from situation to situation. It is often tenuous and easily influenced by events and other people. The more your self-esteem depends on external factors, such as people's approval, status, being loved, or wealth, the more vulnerable you are to loss of self-esteem.

Self-esteem is strongly related to mood. When self-esteem is high, you feel good; when self-esteem is low, you feel bad. More specifically, I believe that **self-esteem and depression are inversely related**; when self-esteem declines, depression increases.

The Development of Self-Esteem

Early in life, we are greatly influenced by other people's opinions of us. This is particularly true of people who are important to us, such as our parents. Since children are unable to distinguish opinions from facts, we accept what people tell us as fact. Therefore, their opinions of us often define us.

Although direct messages from significant adults are important in shaping the child's self-perception, indirect messages from which the child infers personal attributes may be even more important. So if a parent tells her child, "You are smart," the child may accept that as a factual description of herself. She is even more likely to do so, however, if she hears her mother tell one of her friends, "My daughter is so smart!" Furthermore, the way that important adults treat the child conveys powerful messages about how the child is perceived, which become part of the child's self-concept. So if the mother in the previous example says to her daughter, "I'd like your thinking on making up today's shopping list; you're so good at that sort of thing," this reinforces the child's growing sense of being a competent person.

The child's emerging self-concept need not involve self-esteem. Self-concept refers to who we are; self-esteem refers to our self-worth. It is only when we apply the Osiris Factor to our self-concept that self-esteem emerges. For example, if I think of myself as weighing 150 pounds and having grey hair, that is part of my self-concept. But if I tell myself that this is bad, that I *should* weigh less and still have blond hair, then I am judging these attributes and that influences my self-esteem.

When adults compare their perceptions of the child with their beliefs of how the child should be (that is, comparing their Perceived World with their Fantasy World regarding the child) they approve or disapprove of the child and his or her actions. These judgments are gradually internalized by the child and become the basis of his or her self-esteem. For example, if weighing more than peers is judged by adults to be wrong, bad, undesirable, and so forth, the child's self-esteem will decline with increasing weight. If being "beautiful" is judged as good and desirable, the child's self-esteem will decline as physical beauty (as judged by herself and/or others) wanes.

As the child ages, he develops his own Fantasy World of how he "should" be. He then constantly compares his self-perceptions with this fantasy. These comparisons determine his self-esteem. The child's beliefs of how he should be are not necessarily an accurate reproduction of the messages received from important adults. They are the child's interpretation of these messages, which can involve significant distortions. Furthermore, society constantly strengthens some messages and weakens others. Throughout our life, we are exposed to a bombardment of messages of how we should look, act, think, feel, and so on. Since many of these messages are based on irrational beliefs, they set us up for loss of self-esteem as we compare our self-perceptions with the Fantasy World that has been thrust upon us. A review of beliefs about self presented in chapter three will illustrate popular irrational Fantasy World beliefs by which we are likely to judge ourselves.

When others judge us, we may accept their opinions as valid and let them influence our self-esteem. Many people's self-judgments tend to be negative, but they may seek constant reassurance from others to neutralize the internal criticisms. For example, Jill works diligently at improving her physical attractiveness, exercising compulsively, applying expensive makeup, and occasionally resorting to cosmetic surgery. She then seeks relationships with people who will validate her attractiveness. Without this external validation, however, she becomes hypercritical of her appearance, loses self-esteem, and becomes increasingly desperate for approval.

You might think that, as a child matures, he would realize that other people's opinions are not facts. He could then revise his self-esteem from more realistic assessments of himself.

Unfortunately, most adults continue to confuse opinions and facts, so that they often remain vulnerable to other people's opinions. Many adults' self-esteem rises or falls in response to the messages they receive from others. If their mate tells them that they're wonderful, they feel great about themselves. But if their mate suggests that they are worms, their self-esteem plummets.

The idea that we have child members of our internal committee which continue to function throughout our lives helps to explain this peculiar vulnerability. As discussed in chapter nine, these parts of us continue to confuse opinions with facts. Our mature adult parts may realize that someone calling us stupid does not lower our intelligence. But our child parts may react with loss of self-esteem. This would be particularly likely if, as a child, we developed the belief that we were stupid. So early beliefs about ourselves can have major impact on our lives as adults.

Mack, a forty-year-old man, recently consulted me to help overcome intense anxiety when taking tests. He could not complete an engineering degree because he could not pass tests. Although intelligent, he reported that when taking tests, he panicked and could not think. He would have to reread questions several times before he could even understand them.

Questioning revealed that Mack had not had this problem with tests while in the military, where he had done well. He recognized that the tests were no different, but his attitude while taking them was entirely different. As a military man, he felt confident and could think clearly while taking tests. As a civilian, he felt inadequate and stupid, and could not think well while taking tests.

In therapy, Mack was surprised to discover that, when he imagined himself in a test situation, he had a vivid memory of a scene when he was seven or eight years old. He saw himself cowering over a homework assignment as his father berated him for being stupid and told him that he would never learn anything. He connected this scene with many others in which his father had given him similar messages. The feelings he had while taking tests were the same feelings he recalled from his childhood when his father criticized him for his "stupidity."

Mack's case illustrates how inconsistently we can act from different committee members. In military settings, Mack functioned from an adult committee member; he felt competent, thought clearly, and did well. In a civilian setting, he functioned from a scared child committee member. He felt stupid and scared, thought as a child, and did poorly.

Self-Confidence

Self-esteem can influence self-confidence. Whereas self-esteem refers to how we judge ourselves as a person, self-confidence refers to **how well we think we can function.** People with low self-esteem usually have low self-confidence. Since they think poorly of themselves, they doubt their ability to function well and succeed.

Most people think of self-confidence globally. They either have high self-confidence, or they have low self-confidence. But since self-confidence refers to how we assess our ability to do well and succeed, to be realistic it must vary from task to task. We may have high self-confidence in some tasks and low self-confidence in other tasks. For example, I have very high self-confidence in my ability to drive a car, lower self-confidence in my ability to pilot a plane (because I haven't flown much lately), and very low self-confidence in my ability to play a violin (I have never played one, and I am a musical ignoramus).

To avoid having generally low self-confidence, **think**

specifically. Realize that you will have different levels of self-confidence, depending on the specific task with which you are dealing.

Also consider that self-confidence is a **matter of degree**. Thinking in terms of all/nothing, either/or, black/white distinctions leads to erroneous conclusions. Making a rough estimate (perhaps expressed as a percentage) of how well you can do specific tasks avoids the global approach. For example, I estimate my self-confidence in my driving ability at 95%, my self-confidence in my piloting ability at 90%, and so on.

With this approach, self-confidence regarding specific tasks can vary from time to time. With practice, special training, and so on, proficiency with a task usually improves. Fatigue, illness, lack of practice, and so on usually reduce level of performance.

Don't strive for high self-confidence in all situations. It would be unrealistic, and it could lead to disappointment or even to danger. Suppose, for example, that I have generalized high self-confidence, and that I have the strange belief that I can do anything! Suppose that I decide to do some downhill skiing. Though I might never have skied before, glowing with self-confidence, I might tackle a challenging ski run. I might then plunge confidently down the mountain to a catastrophe. Or taking a less extreme example, suppose that I decide to become a violin virtuoso. Since I have high self-confidence and believe that I can do anything I set my mind to, I take lessons, practice, and so on. I fully expect to be fiddling with the best of them in short order. Bad news! Since I am tone deaf and have poor fine motor coordination, my goal of becoming a good violinist is doomed to failure.

All of us have limitations; we have strengths, and we have weaknesses. To believe that we can succeed at anything we choose will set us up for failure (Fantasy World strikes again!).

Therefore, **aim for a realistic level of self-confidence**, not for a uniformly high level.

Raising Self-Esteem

Many people yearn for high self-esteem. They want to think of themselves as terrific human beings who can accomplish anything. But research has found that excessively high self-esteem is as destructive as excessively low self-esteem (American Psychiatric Association, 1994). People with unusually high self-esteem are often grandiose and selfish. They may also be insensitive to the feelings of others and try to gratify their own needs without consideration of others. Like self-confidence, it seems that people do best when their self-esteem is **realistic**, neither too high nor too low. Although striving for a realistic level of self-esteem may be a valid goal, as you will soon read, I prefer a more basic solution.

Since most people suffer from low rather than high self-esteem, I'll focus on ways of increasing self-esteem. Furthermore, people who have excessively high self-esteem seldom want to change. They are usually satisfied with themselves but often make life miserable for others.

Raising self-esteem requires reversing the factors that contributed to its loss. Think of it as reprogramming the mental computer. Since low self-esteem often results from being bombarded by criticisms, you can raise self-esteem by **increasing the positive messages** that you receive and accept. Unless you accept positive messages, they will have no impact on self-esteem. Many people have such negative beliefs about themselves that they automatically discount positive messages. If I believe that I am a Total Worm, when someone comments on the pretty colors of my wings (seeing me as a butterfly), I'll conclude that they're blind, crazy, ingratiating, manipulative, and so forth. In some way, I'll destroy their positive message. Unless I am willing to accept positive messages at face value, they'll be wasted. They will not affect my self-esteem.

But how can we get positive messages? Fortunately, there are several simple ways of **increasing our intake of positive messages**. Consider the following tactics:

- **Spend time with people who give positive messages**; avoid people who specialize in negative criticisms and discounts.
- **Reward people for giving you positive messages**. Say "thank you," or "I appreciate that." Or in some other way let them know that you welcome their messages (for example, smile). Nothing discourages people from giving positive messages more than having their messages discounted (example: Someone tells me, "You're looking really good today," and I reply "You must be blind, I've never looked worse.")
- **Ask people for positive input**. Let the people who are important to you know that you like getting positive messages from them. A good time to do this is when they have given you such a message. For example, when your mate compliments your cooking, you might say, "It's really nice of you to praise me that way. It's very important to me to get compliments from you; it really feels good!"
- **Make mental movies of positive messages**, so that you can replay them to remind yourself of the good feelings they generated. Then validate the messages by telling yourself "Yes!" or "I really deserved that!" and so on.
- **Learn to give yourself positive messages**. The

better you get at this skill, the less you will be dependent on others for maintaining self-esteem. You might begin by **writing down at least five of your accomplishments during the past day** each evening. Be sure to recognize modest accomplishments (such as getting out of bed, feeding the cat, and so on). Develop the habit of **giving yourself positive messages throughout the day**, at every opportunity. Compliment yourself for small positive steps. For example, I give myself an "attaboy" for exercising, for shaving, and so on.

- **When self-esteem is undermined by internal negative "don't" messages, give yourself powerful permissions.** A permission, in this context, means an internal message which allows you to do something which is forbidden by an internal prohibition. If you have a prohibition against acting like a child, for example, an appropriate permission might be, "It's all right to be a child at the appropriate place and time." If you have been laboring under a "don't think" internal message, you might tell yourself, "It's fine to think, and I can do it well!" Don't expect to feel comfortable with these messages until you have repeated them often, with conviction! Likewise, don't expect to feel comfortable, nor to be skilled, when acting on new permissions. Remember that replacing old habits with new ones takes practice, time, and effort.
- **To replace negative internal messages about you as a person (such as "I'm lazy," "I'm selfish," and so forth), develop positive self-affirmations**—that is, positive descriptions of yourself to replace the old negative self-descriptions.

Suppose that you grew up with the belief that "I am stupid." You might replace this belief with a new affirmation that "I am intelligent, and I can learn well and solve difficult problems." Once you are satisfied with the wording of the self-affirmations, write them down on 3X5" cards. Then place them where you'll often see them daily (for example, on your night stand, attached to the refrigerator, on the dash of your car, and so forth). Make a habit of **repeating the self-affirmations with conviction every time you see the cards**. Even more importantly, repeat the appropriate self-affirmation every time that the old negative belief surfaces. For example, suppose that when you begin to read a difficult book, you think, "I won't understand this, because I am stupid." Immediately tell yourself, "No, I am intelligent, and I can learn easily and well!" You probably won't believe the new affirmations at first, though you might realize they are logical. Repetition of the new beliefs with conviction will gradually increase their power and credibility. Eventually you will believe them as strongly as you believed the old negative garbage.

- **If you are spiritually inclined, get in the habit of reminding yourself often that you are the creation of a Higher Power**. This means that you are inherently worthwhile and precious. Depending on your spiritual beliefs, you can probably find **specific scriptures** that will illustrate this idea. Write down the selected scriptures, and recite them daily.
- **Develop the habit of using trances positively to enhance self-esteem**. As discussed earlier, everyone goes in and out of altered states of consciousness (trances) during which they run internal movies. People

with low self-esteem often go into negative trances, in which they see themselves negatively. For example, they may review repeatedly experiences of failure, humiliation, abuse, and so forth. These internal movies usually reinforce negative beliefs about themselves. For example, a person who believes that she is stupid will tend to rerun movies of situations in which she acted stupidly. You can learn to reverse this process, replacing negative movies with positive ones. Instead of reviewing experiences in which you acted stupidly, for example, run internal movies of experiences in which you acted intelligently. If you can't recall suitable experiences, create new movies in which you experience the desired positive quality.

- **Develop rituals as a powerful way of changing negative beliefs about yourself to positive beliefs.** A ritual is a symbolic ceremony to foster or to celebrate a change. Examples of common rituals in our culture include marriage, birthday, graduation, funeral, and so forth. Use your creativity to design one or more rituals to reinforce changes in your self-esteem. For example, Jane wrote on slips of paper each negative belief about herself she had discovered. These beliefs included, "I am unworthy of love," "I can't measure up," "I'll never succeed in relationships," and so forth. She then invited good friends to join her for a ritual. She read each belief and then threw the slip of paper on which it was written into a roaring fire in her fireplace. As each slip burned, she told her friends the new belief that replaced the old one. Her friends reinforced each new belief with positive comments, including their experiences of Jane, which confirmed the new belief.

The End of Self-Esteem

Raising self-esteem will not solve the self-esteem issue. You will continue to be vulnerable to depression, guilt, and shame, *as long as you operate from the Osiris Factor and judge yourself.* The ultimate solution to self-esteem issues is to stop judging yourself. **Replace the Osiris Factor with the Humility Factor**, and free yourself of guilt, shame, depression, and anger.

By operating from the Humility Factor, you accept yourself as you are. I call this the **Popeye Model** of self-esteem. You may recall that Popeye was a fictitious comic book sailor who had a wonderful saying. It was something like this: "I am what I am, and that's all that I am." That is a nonjudgmental approach to oneself, which is impossible from the Osiris Factor. Popeye had no self-esteem problems.

When asked for my level of self-esteem, I respond that I don't do self-esteem anymore. By this, I mean that I no longer judge myself; I accept myself as I am. It does not mean that I like everything about me. There are many things about me that I do not like, things that I wish were different. But that doesn't mean that they *should* be different; it means that I would *prefer* it if they were different. Nor does this mean that I approve of everything that I do. Like most mortals, I make my share of mistakes. But I don't beat myself up about it. Instead, I ask myself "What can I *learn* from that mistake? How might I *do it differently* in the future?" As a result, mistakes have become useful learning experiences instead of reasons for guilt, shame, and depression.

When I discover one of the (many) things that I don't like about myself, I ask myself two questions: "Can I realistically change this aspect of myself?" and "If I can change it, do I choose to spend the time and effort that would be required?"

We can't change everything we might wish to change about ourselves. For example, I would like to become a good dancer. But my serious limitations in the basic biological requirements of a dancer (such as a good sense of rhythm) make this goal unrealistic. Denying our limitations leads to disappointment and wasted time and effort. And the Fantasy World belief that we can accomplish anything sets us up for guilt ("I didn't try hard enough," and so forth) and shame ("There's something wrong with me for not succeeding," and so on).

There are many things that I would like to change about myself which I could change, but I choose not to change them. The desired change is not worth, to me, the required time and/or effort. For example, I wish that I could speak more languages, but I don't want to spend the time and effort required to learn them.

It might be argued that guilt and shame are the necessary results of a healthy conscience. Without them, we would be psychopaths operating solely on the basis of our needs and desires. In my experience, however, guilt and shame usually do not prevent people from acting in ways which they deem to be unacceptable. They continue to violate their conscience, even though they feel guilt and/or shame. They just feel depressed about it. Sometimes, as in the case of addictions, the depression then leads to an increase in the unacceptable behavior, in an effort to feel better.

Instead of thinking of conscience as an internal source of punishment, I think of conscience as consisting of our moral and ethical beliefs, which become part of our core goals. Rather than asking ourselves whether our actions are right or wrong, we then ask ourselves whether our actions are working or not working with regard to achieving these goals. If what we are doing is sabotaging our goals, the solution is not to blame ourselves and generate guilt and/or shame; it is to change our behavior so as to progress toward our goals. Guilt and shame will often *reduce* our ability to make such changes.

If you are still clinging to the grandiosity of the Osiris Factor, you might contend that your moral and ethical beliefs are "right," and therefore that you "should" follow them (as should everyone else!). Operating from the Humility Factor, on the other hand, you would consider that your moral and ethical beliefs are your *preferences* about important issues in life, based on your early conditioning, cultural influences, and so forth. You would accept that moral and ethical beliefs that differ from your own are no better or no worse; they are just different. And you choose to live your life based on your beliefs. You are also open to reevaluating these beliefs and to changing them. It's your choice.

ELEVEN

LIFE WITHOUT THE OSIRIS FACTOR

In this final chapter I summarize how life can be different when you replace the Osiris Factor with the Humility Factor—when you accept that you are human and not God.

Beliefs

Our beliefs about how things should be (Fantasy World) and about how things are (Perceived World) are not only more realistic when using the Humility Factor, but, more importantly, our beliefs about our beliefs are different. We think of them as personal preferences rather than as facts or self-evident truths. Here are some examples of statements we might make about our beliefs, operating without the Osiris Factor:

- I have beliefs about how I would like things to be, including beliefs about relationships, other people, the world in general, and myself. These beliefs are my personal preferences at this time, and they may change with experience and increased wisdom.
- My beliefs about how I would like things to be contain my moral and ethical preferences, including spiritual and/or religious beliefs. These beliefs underlie most of my core goals.
- My beliefs about how I would like things to be are no better or worse than other people's beliefs about these issues.

- I perceive and remember experiences in my unique way, which is flawed and subject to bias and selectivity.
- "Truth" is my honest assessment of my perceptions and memories, and it is not reality. My truth is not inherently more nor less accurate than the "truth" of others.

Feelings

Feelings enrich life and are a useful source of information. Anger tells us that we want to change something. Sadness informs us of an important loss (grief), that things are not going the way we would like them to go in our life (unhappiness), and/or that we are dissatisfied with ourselves (depression). Anxiety signifies a perceived danger. The glad feelings let us know that we are experiencing things that we would like to occur more often.

The Osiris Factor is responsible for generating two classes of negative feelings which are not useful and which tend to interfere with reaching our goals. These feelings are anger and depression (including shame and guilt). By freeing ourselves of the Osiris Factor, we greatly decrease these negative, counterproductive feelings.

Will we be totally free of anger, guilt, shame, and depression? Probably not. Old habits do not disappear. They may resurface unexpectedly, and sometimes without apparent cause. When they do, we can, if we know how and if we choose to do so, recognize them and replace them with habits that we prefer.

Since anger and depression have complex and powerful physiological aspects, some people may, even after replacing the Osiris Factor with the Humility Factor, retain a physiological vulnerability to these emotions. Nonetheless, operating from the Humility Factor will greatly reduce the frequency, intensity, and duration of these negative emotions. And appropriate biological interventions (such as medication, vigorous exercise, proper sleep and nutrition, etc.) can help to neutralize physiological predispositions and imbalances.

Forgiveness

Relinquishing the Osiris Factor leads to forgiveness. By forgiveness, I do not mean forgetting or validating a past action which we disliked and/or which conflicted with our values. Forgetting such actions is unrealistic. Validating them is often irrational, since it would run counter to our beliefs and/or preferences.

Forgiveness occurs when we **stop repeatedly telling ourselves that someone was wrong and should not have acted as they did**. It is an internal process, which may or may not involve another person. We can forgive ourselves, thereby reducing guilt and/or shame, and we can forgive others, thereby reducing anger. We may or may not tell another person that we have forgiven him; that is not the important issue. What is important is that we stop operating from the Osiris Factor, keeping ourselves upset (angry, guilty, shamed, and/or depressed) by insisting on the wrongness of a past action.

Forgiveness benefits the person doing the forgiving. It frees her of negative emotions. It can also free her from attachment to another person. As long as we generate anger toward another, that person controls part of our life by dominating our thoughts and feelings. Forgiving that person severs that emotional bond. We are then free to abandon the relationship or to resume it without anger. That is our choice. Forgiveness does not mean that we are compelled to maintain a relationship with the person whom we have forgiven.

Relationships

When we use the Humility Factor, relationships are free of criticism, contempt, defensiveness, and anger. We accept other people as they are, without judging them or insisting that they should change to meet our Fantasy World. We no longer require them to perceive and remember things as we do.

Instead of dissipating energy on anger, we calmly tell others of changes we would like them to make, and we then ask them if they are willing to make the changes. If they refuse, we accept their decision without blaming them. Based on that information, we decide if we wish to continue the relationship, and, if so, how we might choose to modify it.

Violence is virtually impossible from the Humility Factor, since we no longer anger ourselves and do not judge others. Only defensive violence might occur, not because we judge another wrong, but because we choose to protect others or ourselves from injury or death. Wars become unlikely, since countries no longer judge other countries as wrong. Most people will only go to war and risk their safety and that of their loved ones if they feel strongly that they are fighting righteously against an evil foe. Propaganda is a tool by which a country's leaders convince its citizens of the wrongness of the enemy and the righteousness of their own cause. Prejudice and its related abominations likewise disappear in a world no longer under the domination of the Osiris Factor, since it is based on negative judgments of groups of people.

BIBLIOGRAPHY

American Psychiatric Association. (1994). *Diagnostic and statistical manual of mental disorders (4th ed.)*. Washington, D.C.: Author.

Beck, A., Rush, J., Shaw, B., & Emery, G. (1979). *Cognitive therapy of depression*. New York: Guilford.

Beck, A., Wright, F., Newman, C., Liese, B. (1993). *Cognitive therapy of substance abuse*. New York: The Guilford Press.

Berne, E. (1961). *Transactional analysis in psychotherapy*. New York: Random House, Inc.

Berne, E. (1972). *What do you say after you say hello*. New York: Grove Press, Inc.

Borg, M. (2001). *Reading the Bible again for the first time*. New York: HarperCollins Publishers, Inc.

Bowlby, J. (1973). *Attachment and loss, Vol. 2. Separation: anxiety and anger*. New York: Basic Books.

Brennan, B. (1987). *Hands of light*. New York: Bantom.

Burns, F. (1981). *Feeling good*. New York: Signet.

Cade, B., & O'Hanlon, W. H. (1993). *A brief guide to brief therapy*. New York: W. W. Norton & Company.

Carpenter, S (2001). Sights unseen. *Monitor on Psychology*, 32, 52-57.

Chopra, D. (1993). *Ageless body, timeless mind*. New York: Harmony Books.

Clay, R. (1996). Psychologists' faith in religion begins to grow. *Monitor*, August.

de Shazer, S. (1985). *Keys to solution in brief therapy*. New York: W.W. Norton & Company.

dc Shazer, S. (1988). *Clues.* New York: W.W. Norton & Company.

Ellis, A. (1994). *Reason and emotion in psychotherapy.* Revised and updated. New York: Carol Publishing Group.

Ellis, A. (1995). *Better, deeper, and more enduring brief therapy.* New York: Brunner/Mazel.

Ellis, A., McInerney, J.F., Di Guiseppe, R., & Yeager, R.J. (1988). *Rational-emotive therapy with alcoholics and substance abusers.* Boston, MA: Allyn and Bacon.

Gallup Organization (1991). *Sleep in America.* Princeton, N.J.: Author.

Garber, J., & Seligman, M. (Eds.). (1980). *Human helplessness.* Orlando, FA: Academic Press, Inc.

Goleman, D., & Gurin, J. (Eds.). (1996). *Mind body medicine.* Yonkers, N.Y.: Consumer Reports Books.

Gordon, J.S. (1996). *Manifesto for a new medicine.* Reading, MA: Addison-Wesley Publishing Company, Inc.

Hammond, C., et al. (1994). *Clinical hypnosis and memory: guidelines for clinicians and for forensic hypnosis.* Des Plaines, IL: American Society of Clinical Hypnosis Press.

Hauri, P., & Linde, S. (1991). *No more sleepless nights.* New York: Wiley.

Hollon, S.D., De Rubeis, R.J., Evans, M.D., Wiemer, M., Garvey, M.J., Grove, W.M., & Tuason, V.B. (1992). Cognitive therapy and pharmacotherapy for depression: singly and in combination. *Archives of General Psychiatry,* 49, 774-781.

Institute of Noetic Sciences. 475 Gate Five Road, Suite 300. Sausalito, CA 94965.

Isthmus Institute. 2701 State Street.Dallas. TX, 75204.

Johnson, D. (2001). Polling the planet. *The Futurist*, March-April 2001, 12-13.

Kabat-Zinn, J. (1991). *Full catastrophe living*. New York: Dell Publishing.

Krieger, D. (1977). *The therapeutic touch: how to use your hands to help or heal.* Englewood Cliffs, NJ: Prentice-Hall.

Lerner, H. (1985). *The dance of anger*. New York: Harper & Row.

Locke, S., & Colligan, D. (1986). *The healer within*. New York: E.P. Dutton.

Loftus, E., & Ketcham, K. (1991). *Witness for the defense*. New York: St. Martin's Press.

Maultsby, M. (1984). *Rational behavior therapy*. Englewood Cliffs, NJ: Prentice-Hall.

Murphy, M., & White, R.A. (1978). *In the zone*. New York: Penguin Books.

Newton, R. (1993). *What makes nature tick*? Cambridge, MA: Harvard University Press.

Nideffer, R.M. (1992). *Psyched to win*. Champaign, IL: Leisure Press.

O'Connor, E. (2001). Can't get no satisfaction? *Monitor on psychology*, 32, 13.

Ornish, D. (1990). *Dr. Dean Ornish's program for reversing heart disease: the only system scientifically proven to reverse heart disease without drugs or surgery*. New York: Random House.

Peck, M.S. (1978). *The road less traveled*. New York: Simon & Schuster.

Pendergrast, M. (1995). *Victims of memory: incest accusations and shattered lives.* Hinesberg, VT: Upper Access, Inc.

Rossi, E. (1986). *The psychobiology of mind-body healing.* New York: W.W. Norton & Co., Inc.

Sears, B. (1995). *Enter the zone.* New York: Harper Collins Publishers, Inc.

Seligman, M. (1975). *Helplessness.* San Francisco, CA: W.H. Freeman and Company.

Siegman, A., & Dembroski, T.M. (Eds.). (1989). *In search of coronary-prone behavior: beyond type A.* Hillsdale, NJ.: Lawrence Erlbaum Associates.

Skinner, B.F. (1938). *The behavior of organisms: an experimental analysis.* New York: Appleton-Century-Crofts.

Steiner, C. (1974). *Scripts people live.* New York: Grove Press, Inc.

Stern, D.N. (1985). *The interpersonal world of the infant: a view from psychoanalysis and developmental psychology.* New York: Basic Books.

The National Institute for the Clinical Application of Behavioral Medicine. (1991). *The psychology of health, immunity, and disease.* Mansfield, CT: The National Institute for the Clinical Application of Behavioral Medicine.

Tripey, J. (1989). *The small book.* New York: Delacorte Press.

Viorst, J. (1986). *Necessary losses.* New York: Ballantine Books.

Williams, R. (1989). *The trusting heart: great news about type A behavior.* New York: Times Books.

Yapko, M. (1994). *Suggestions of abuse.* New York: Simon & Schuster.

INDEX

ABOUT THE AUTHOR

Dr. Philip Roos is a licensed clinical psychologist providing individual, couple, and family therapy. He consults with sixty police and fire departments, as well as with nursing homes.

He has served as the National Executive Director of the ARC (Association for Retarded Citizens) and of MADD (Mothers Against Drunk Driving). He has also held top state-level positions in New York and Texas and has held several academic appointments with major universities. He operated flight schools as a commercial flight instructor in planes and gliders.

In his youth, he played polo and trained polo ponies, and he is currently training his young Arabian horse, Cheatin Heart. He lives in Arlington, Texas, with his wife, Dr. Susan Roos, and with two cats.

9 26575 75953 5